Dialogues
with Children

Dialogues with Children

Gareth B. Matthews

HARVARD UNIVERSITY PRESS
Cambridge, Massachusetts
and London, England

Copyright © 1984 by the President
and Fellows of Harvard College
All rights reserved
Printed in the United States of America
10 9 8 7 6 5 4 3 2

First Harvard University Press paperback edition, 1992

Library of Congress Cataloging in Publication Data

Matthews, Gareth B., 1929–
  Dialogues with children.

  1. Children and philosophy.   I. Title.
B105.C45M36 1984   108'.80544   84-6578
ISBN 0-674-20284-8

For Andrea
Daniel
David-Paul
Donald
Esther
Martin
Neil
Richard

Contents

Foreword

by Robert Coles

IN MY MANY YEARS of working with children in America and abroad, I have occasionally heard a child speak with astonishing wit and canniness. Or I have heard a child ask a question that has perplexed me, even taken me aback with surprise. Later I would think about what I'd heard and be grateful for it—a chance, yet again, to learn from others, to be helped to ask a question, ponder a riddle. But such encounters with boys and girls have also prompted other reactions in me: confusion, alarm, irritation, resentment—to the point that the especially stimulating encounters of the kind Gareth Matthews describes have become, at times, ordeals for me.

I refer to the skepticism of many adults with respect to these "dialogues" or human conversational exchanges—doubt that they are possible or that they have any larger intellectual or moral significance. In the course of writing up my own studies I have repeatedly found myself doubting that children are capable of powerfully stated observations, of sustained eloquence, never mind moral reflection and analysis. But that is just what Matthews offers us, through the words of particular boys and girls, both in his first book, *Philosophy and the Young Child*, and now in this one. How to account for this skepticism, this outright refusal (by some rather authoritative figures in our intellectual tradition, and, of course, by those of us who heed them) to acknowledge capabilities demonstrated time and again to Matthews and, one dares say, to countless thousands of parents and teachers?

In *Philosophy and the Young Child* Matthews attempted to answer that question. He pointed out that a number of theorists of "child development" and of "moral development" don't regard children in the same light his books would encourage in us. Such theorists do not really relax and talk with children day after day; rather, they ask them pointed questions, get them to perform tasks, then grade them. Yet the theorists live rather persistently in my mind, to the point that the emotions mentioned above still keep pressing upon me as I work. In fact, my wife, who is a schoolteacher, and I have a standing dialogue of our own in consequence of this continuing dilemma. After hearing a child—one of our sons or a boy or girl we have come to know in our field work—say something perceptive, we comment to each other, "But children aren't supposed to talk like that!"

The most important and revealing moment in my own research took place two decades ago when I got to know fairly well a black child of six who had to endure unspeakable hate, constant threats, and insults as she marched daily past menacing mobs assembled to obstruct her effort to integrate a New Orleans elementary school. I was certain that soon she would begin to fall apart emotionally. The entire school, after all, had been abandoned because white parents refused to let their sons and daughters attend classes in a building where this one child happened also to be. Federal marshals had to escort her past these mobs, and their all too evident fury seemed likely to overwhelm a vulnerable mind.

Yet the child held her head high, survived her tormentors, astonished a federal judge, a schoolteacher, a principal, and any number of us who couldn't quite comprehend her constant cheerfulness, her pluck, her determination and, not least, her compassionate charity, as she announced herself willing to pray for her hecklers. When I asked this girl why she would pray for such people, she replied quietly but firmly, "Because they need praying for." I prodded her again, why, and she replied, "Because Jesus told us to feel sorry for the people who talk like that." When I asked her to offer her sources, so to speak, for that kind of Biblical exegesis— "Jesus *did*?"—I received my reply rather promptly. "He did, yes, when he was dying, and he asked God to forgive the people who were killing him."

Now such an interpretation was well within this child's analytic and reflective capacity, but I was not then ready to say so, and even now I remind myself that she may have been repeating what others had told her (as if the rest of us, grown up and with degrees of one kind or another, don't do just this when we quote authorities and experts and draw from texts). What this New Orleans child had really done was what the children in Matthews's book also do: she had looked and listened, then used her mind to ask, to reflect, and come up with some answers. These fellow human beings, she had decided, are truly awful, but the Bible tells us it has been like this before, even for Jesus himself. She told herself to remember that, to follow his example as closely as possible, and she succeeded in so doing.

The children in this book are in that tradition. They are anxious to pursue their humanity as members of a species whose essential nature is displayed on every page of this book. Children, like others called "human beings," summon language in the interests of continuing awareness, in the form of a constant curiosity, an imagination always at work, a full-fledged reflective energy. They join those of us who are older in a desire to edify, to reach others with their messages.

As Matthews indicates, children are quite willing, in their pursuit of understanding, to ask sensible, provocative questions. They persist earnestly with those questions until some cognitive and moral hunger is appeased—unless they figure out that the adults around them have no wish to hear what is on their minds. So the "dialogues" here are no miraculous product of a one-in-a-million exchange, but rather are culled from a sensitive father's, a knowing teacher's, everyday experience. They have their echoes, surely, in all of our lives, if we would but stop and remember, stop and notice and, not least, join a child's proposed colloquy.

Acknowledgments

THIS BOOK was written while I was on a fellowship from the National Endowment for the Humanities. I thank the Endowment for that assistance.

Parts of several chapters first appeared in an article in *Phenomenology + Pedagogy* 1 (1983), and in a review of *Wally's Stories*, by Vivian Gussin Paley, in *Thinking* 3 (1981–82). I thank the editors of those journals for permission to use that material.

I thank Edward Wieringa for passing on to me an important anecdote. I thank the School of Epistemics of Edinburgh University, and especially its director, Barry Richards, for kind and generous hospitality during the year in which this book was written. I also thank the headmaster of St. Mary's Music School, J. P. S. Allison, without whose kind cooperation the events recorded here would not have taken place.

Prologue

TALKING TO CHILDREN is nothing new. As parents, grandparents, teachers, neighbors, and casual acquaintances, we talk to children all the time. Sometimes our aim is practical. We urge them to wash behind their ears, to watch less TV, to change their clothes when they get home from school. Often our aim is pedagogical. We want them to learn how to tie their shoes, to say the three-times table, to improve their spelling or grammar. Sometimes our aim is social. We want our children to respect their elders and to get along with other children.

If we are psychologists, we may talk to children to find out how they perform at a particular age. We may view what they say as an indication of how they are developing, perhaps even of how children in a certain age group normally develop, and of why normal development sometimes fails to take place. If we are teachers or parents, we may talk to children to find out whether their development is on schedule.

What we adults don't do, when we talk to children,

is discuss matters we ourselves find difficult or problematic. How could a child, a mere child, make a useful contribution to thinking about something that we, with our much greater maturity and experience, find difficult or elusive? Why should a child be interested in such matters anyway? Don't children have enough to think about that is "on their own level"? If we adults show children that we don't know all the answers, perhaps don't even know where to look for answers, won't that disturb and upset them? Isn't it crucial to their emotional well-being to believe, even if wrongly, that their parents and teachers know the answers to any difficulties a child can think of?

Most adults act as though all the questions in the last paragraph were merely rhetorical, questions whose answers are so obvious that the very act of asking them has the force of answering them. The pages that follow are meant to show otherwise.

The title of this book, *Dialogues with Children*, may suggest to some readers that I am offering evidence to support one theory of child development or to criticize another. Indeed, I do have something to say later on about how the dialogues bear on theories of cognitive development. But it is not primarily as data for psychological theorizing that I present the record of these conversations.

Some readers may suppose that a book with this title will be a how-to-do-it guide for conducting interesting conversations with children. Certainly I would be pleased if parents and teachers found some of my methods helpful in developing their own dialogues with children. But emphasizing the techniques puts things the wrong way around.

My first aim is to interest adults in a range of fascinating questions that they can profitably reflect on with children, questions that should not be considered the exclusive province of professional philosophers. My second aim is to portray, as attractively as I can, the possibility of having a relationship with children that is different from any my readers are likely to be used to. This relationship is one without condescension—without the condescension of experimenter to subject, or of instructor to neophyte, or of loving provider to recipient of care. Of course I have no wish to denigrate the value of conducting experiments with children, or of giving them instruction, or of looking after their welfare. But the importance of those tasks, and the difficulties that stand in the way of performing them well, have been detailed and emphasized by many others.

What has not been taken seriously, or even widely conceived, is the possibility of tackling with children, in a relationship of mutual respect, the naively profound questions of philosophy. I hope that what follows will convince my readers that children can help us adults investigate and reflect on interesting and important questions and that the children's contributions may be quite as valuable as any we adults have to offer.

Happiness

"Aunt Gertie's flowers are happy again," Freddie reported.

"Flowers can't be happy," scowled Alice, in the corner, hunched over a bowl of cornflakes. "Aunt Gertie likes to talk about flowers as if they were people. But really they don't have any feelings. They can't be thirsty, or sad, or happy."

"Is that right, Mum?" asked Freddie in some disappointment.

"You'd better talk to your Aunt Gertie," said Mother, "she knows much more about flowers than any of the rest of us."

So began a story I made up for a class of eight-to-eleven-year-old children at St. Mary's Music School in Edinburgh, Scotland, in October of 1982. I was spending the academic year at the School of Epistemics in the University of Edinburgh. My project involved doing research into conceptions of childhood and into models of human development, especially cognitive development. I was surrounded by friendly and stimulating colleagues—psychologists, linguists, specialists in artificial intelligence, philosophers—all adults. My research concerned children and how childhood ought to be conceived, but, my own youngest child being almost fifteen, I had no natural associations with any real children.

Thinking it important to remedy this deprivation, I approached the headmaster of St. Mary's Music School, J. P. S. Allison. St. Mary's is a very small, very good school for musically gifted primary and secondary school children. I asked if I could help out once a week in some capacity with the youngest kids. The headmaster, after he had sized me up, gave me permission to do whatever I chose one period a week with the Juniors. It was only after I was given carte blanche in this way that I formulated the project of getting these children to help me write philosophical stories.

Alice's skeptical comments about flowers were meant to start a discussion among the kids, and they did.

The children thought there was no doubt that flowers could be thirsty but they wanted to discuss whether flowers could be happy.

"Why don't you think flowers can be happy?" I asked.

"They haven't got a mind," said Daniel, quickly, clearly, and decisively. At eight and a half, Daniel was, by a day, the youngest member of the class.

"Any other reason?" I asked.

"They have no feelings," he added.

David-Paul, who was ten, then entered the discussion. "There is a plant," he said, "which is constructed so that its leaves can come together and catch flies."

I asked if anyone knew what that plant was called.

"A flytrap," someone said.

We discussed Venus's flytrap for a while.

"You touch it and it curls up," said Ise (pronounced "Eese"), nine and a half.

"That's like a butterfly," Esther put in. At eleven, Esther was the oldest member of the class.

"But isn't it like a reflex?" David-Paul asked. "It's like a spring; when you touch it, it curls up."

I asked whether, if what the sensitive plant does is like the action of a reflex, that means the plant doesn't have any feelings.

"Well, it's got to be sensitive anyway," said Esther. "If it can curl up, it's got to be sensitive."

A discussion developed as to whether flowers can communicate with each other.

"Plants might be able to talk to each other by, you know, radio waves or something like that," suggested David-Paul. "Or by dust that goes from one plant to another."

I asked why it is important, in determining whether something can be happy, to find out if it can talk. It seemed clear to the kids that language could reveal mood. But perhaps, they suggested, mood could be revealed in other ways.

"In a sort of a way the plant shows that it's happy by blooming," David-Paul said. The kids then discussed gestures as the expression of mood or feeling.

Ise worried about the idea that flowers must be unhappy whenever they bow down. "It doesn't necessarily mean you're unhappy if you're bowing down," she pointed out. "You could be in a bad mood just standing up straight."

"Does [a plant] have a brain?" asked Daniel.

I said that his question was a good one and asked why

knowing whether a plant has a brain might help us determine whether plants can be happy.

"Without a brain you couldn't be sad or happy or anything like that," said Martin, who was almost ten. "Without a brain you wouldn't [even] exist."

The second half of Martin's comment triggered off in me a host of questions about life and death (whether, for example, some criterion of lack of brain function might be satisfactory for human death, and whether a human embryo without a functioning brain is really a human being). But before I could formulate a follow-up question, the discussion had moved on.

"I don't really think a plant is saying to itself, 'I'm happy,' 'I'm sad,' " David-Paul said. "It's a kind of machine. It can be active or run down and need more power."

"Do flowers have eyes?" asked Daniel.

"No," said several of the kids.

"But inside, there is something like an eye," Daniel insisted. He seemed to be thinking of the stamen and pistil as an eye on a stalk.

The idea of a plant's needing to see around it tripped off David-Paul. "A nettle," he said, "could feel it's going to get damaged and it needs to protect itself."

Soon our discussion time was up. We had had only half an hour to consider whether flowers could be happy. We certainly hadn't settled the question, but we had canvassed an impressive variety of relevant considerations.

I had promised the kids that the following week I would bring in a conclusion to the story and I would use in it as much as I could of what they had said in class. (They knew I was tape-recording our discussion.) I asked the kids to suggest which of their various comments might go into the mouth of Alice, which would be better said by Aunt Gertie, and so on. They made very reasonable recommendations.

I went home, transcribed the discussion from the tape, and set about using it to complete the story. In fact, using the kids' comments to continue the story was no problem at all. The problem was deciding how to end the story, for our discussion had come to no clear conclusion.

I decided to make up a conclusion of my own. I took Aristotle's discussion of *eudaimonia* ("happiness," as it had traditionally been put, or "human flourishing," as many present-day students of Aristotle prefer to say) from the *Nicomachean Ethics* and applied it to plants. I don't think Aristotle would have been happy with my adaptation, but other scholars might disagree.[1] Anyway, here is the Aristotelian, or pseudo-Aristotelian, ending I invented for the story:

> Freddie decided to confront Aunt Gertie with the flower question. "Aunt Gertie, how do we know that chrysants are happy?"
>
> "Didn't you see them today?" Aunt Gertie asked. "Their faces are all turned up and smiling at us."
>
> "Oh, you just want to pretend they're like people," said Alice sourly. "You know they don't really have any feelings at all. They can't feel happy."
>
> Aunt Gertie straightened up in her chair. "Do you think happiness is a feeling, Alice?" she asked,

---

1. See, for example, his *Eudemian Ethics* 1.7 and his *Nicomachean Ethics* 1.9.

"maybe a warm, gently tickling feeling that spreads over your body?"

"I don't know about that," said Alice cautiously.

"If you think happiness is like the feeling of hot chocolate going down your throat on a cold day, then maybe flowers aren't happy," Aunt Gertie conceded. "So far as we know, they don't have that kind of sensation. But some of your happiest times are when you're doing something you like doing— singing in a big chorus or playing a game well. You don't have time to stop and get warm feelings. Your happiness is just doing something you are good at doing, with all you've got in you. Flowers can hold their heads high and show off their blossoms with all they have in them. When they are healthy and well watered they tend to do that. And that's happiness for a flower."

Freddie thought about what Aunt Gertie had said. One of his happiest moments, he thought, came when he got to sing "O Come All Ye Faithful" in the children's choir on Christmas Eve. He didn't know why he liked that carol so much, but he did. Maybe he had some warm feelings then, but happiness wasn't those warm feelings, or you could be happy by just going over to the gas fire. Maybe happiness for any living thing is just doing something very well, with all you've got in you, as Aunt Gertie had said. For a flower, that would be blooming.

The following week we read the completed story together. There were several appreciative chuckles at the line about going over to the gas fire to become happy.

(The open gas heater in the classroom where we met was much appreciated in Edinburgh's winter, in fact, in Edinburgh's autumn and spring as well—even if it couldn't be guaranteed to make you happy!)

I had put in the bit about singing in a choir to draw on the lives of the choristers in the class. Five of the seven children in the class (and later, when Richard joined us in January, six of eight members) were in the choir of St. Mary's (Scottish Episcopal) Cathedral. (In fact, all the boys, and only the boys, in the class were choristers. The choir was unusual for its tradition of using girl sopranos, as well as boy sopranos, but as it happened, Ise and Esther were violinists rather than choristers.) But I don't really know whether my choice of example was helpful or not.

I asked the children what they thought of the ending. "Good," most of them said cheerfully. "Brilliant," said Daniel, and grinned winningly.

Donald, however, who at ten and a half was obviously a very reflective person, was apparently dissatisfied. He was muttering something I didn't catch at first, so I asked him to repeat it. He liked the story, he said, and thought it was good, but there was a question he still didn't know how to answer, a question that he couldn't get out of his head. He thought flowers could be happy and that what Aunt Gertie said about their being happy when the sun shone was, in a way, quite true. "But," he added with great emphasis, "how can they be happy without a mind? How can they possibly be happy without a mind?" He was not suggesting that I should solve his problem for him or make it go away. He accepted the problem as his own. He would deal with it. I found this response very moving.

Desire

THE STORY about whether flowers can be happy
was the first in a long series of stories I wrote that year
with the help of the Juniors of St. Mary's. I had chosen
the mental life of plants as the topic for our first story
for a particular reason. During the preceding year I had
taught a course on philosophy and children to a group of
about twenty adults, most of whom were schoolteachers
in Boston, Massachusetts. One day I had passed out to
my Boston class copies of this fragment of a conversation
between two kindergartners, from Vivian Paley's *Wally's
Stories*.

Lisa: Do plants wish for baby plants?
Deana: I think only people can make wishes. But
     God could put a wish inside a plant.
Teacher: What would the wish be?
Deana: What if it's a pretty flower? Then God puts

an idea inside to make this plant into a pretty
red flower—if it's supposed to be red.

Teacher: I always think of people having ideas.

Deana: It's just the same. God puts a little idea
in the plant to tell it what to be.

Lisa: My mother wished for me and I came when
it was my birthday.[1]

I asked half the members of my Boston class to write
short papers explaining how they might continue the
conversation with Lisa and Deana. These adults had
been with me long enough to realize that I discouraged
condescension toward young children. With the stimu-
lus of my assignment they were prepared to imagine
discussing with children the notion that a plant might
have an idea or a wish. But they also felt a strong obli-
gation to banish superstition and to disabuse children of
mythical, anthropomorphic and animistic conceptions.
Since they thought it would be obvious to any mature
thinker that plants *really* have neither wishes nor ideas,
they thought children should be "educated" to this
reality.

The papers these adults wrote showed very little sym-
pathy for the notion that a plant might wish for baby
plants or for the suggestion that a plant might develop
according to an idea God had implanted in it. To me
both those notions are very suggestive and very exciting.
In my view, reflecting on those notions is a good way of
trying to get clearer about the nature of plants and the
nature of what we think we know about plants. My ex-

1. Vivian Gussin Paley, *Wally's Stories* (Cambridge, Mass.: Harvard
University Press, 1981), pp. 79–80.

citement and enthusiasm found no echo in the sober and prosaic responses of those adult students. I was disappointed but not discouraged.

Concentrating on the concept of a wish, I tried to convince my students that the concept of a wish is both highly problematic and also quite central to our understanding of the world about us. It is, I said, a notion we (even the "experts" among us) are very confused about, but we don't know how to do without it.

My efforts were largely unsuccessful. Certainly so far as desires and plants were concerned, my students could see no problem. They were willing to allow that one might draw an attractive analogy between the desire-expressing behavior of human beings and certain "actions" of plants, such as producing seeds or putting down roots more deeply in dry weather. But they thought it obvious, and important that it was obvious, that, in the literal sense of "desire," no plant has a desire. Moreover, the obviousness of this "fact" seemed to underline for them the importance of getting children, even quite young children, to accept it.

I went home quite frustrated from that session with my Boston class. In my frustration I wrote a dialogue, and to each of the speeches I affixed the name of a member of my class. At our next meeting I passed out copies of my dialogue and suggested we "perform" it together.

Me: Well, do plants wish for baby plants?
Jane: I have a plant that wants plenty of sunshine and another that really wants shade.
Jean: That's just a way of talking. What you mean

is that the first plant does well in sunshine and the other does better in shade.

Diane: But sometimes plants want to *do* something. For example, I had a morning glory that grew right up the side of the house until it got to the gutter. It bent around the gutter and tried to find a higher place to stick onto. It just wavered around there trying to find a place. It wanted to go higher.

Peter: It has a hormone or something that makes it go up.

Cindy: I know a person who had to take medicine to prevent her from having migraine headaches. The medicine gave her an enormous appetite. Though it was the medicine that gave her the appetite, she really wanted the food.

Peter: Did she *really* want the food?

Cindy: Well, she didn't want to get fat. But even after she had eaten a big meal, she was still hungry.

Me: Having conflicting desires—like wanting food but wanting not to get fat—doesn't mean the desires aren't real.

David: With plants you can always cash in this "want"-talk as tendencies. The morning glory tends to grow up and will do so as long as there is a suitable object for it to adhere to.

Betty: Can't you do that with people, too? A hungry person will tend to eat as long as there is food around.

John: But there is more to it with people. They can *tell* you what they want.

Sally: Sometimes. Sometimes they don't know what

they want. They may have to go to a "shrink" to find out.

Elaine: And what about small babies? When my baby cries three or four hours after the last feeding, she wants milk. She can't tell me that—except by crying.

Marie: Crying is a way of telling somebody you are hungry. When the baby grows up, she'll learn other ways, but crying is a way of telling.

Linda: Couldn't shriveling up your leaves be a way of telling somebody that you want more water? Of course the plant never learns any other way, but maybe shriveling up your leaves is a way of telling somebody you are thirsty.

Shari: From an evolutionary point of view there might even be a similarity. Plants that showed no signs of drying up until they were already dead wouldn't, maybe, get looked after as well as those that did, and so they would fail to propagate. In the same way, babies that didn't cry like bloody murder wouldn't get fed.

Billie Jean: But the main thing that lets us talk about the desires of human babies, even newborns, is that we know the babies will naturally grow up to become human adults who can talk about their own desires. That process of growing up is such a smoothly continuous one that it seems arbitrary to pick a point at which a child first has desires.

Me: But of course there is an analogy between the development of a human individual (ontogeny) and the evolutionary development of the species (phylogeny). The phylogenetic scale exhibits enough continuity that it may seem arbitrary to pick a point along it where there are first real desires. Some things chimps do are like things people do because of desires they have. Some things dogs do are like the "desire"-expressing behavior of chimps. Some things frogs do are like the "desire"-expressing behavior of dogs—and so on, all the way down through animal microorganisms to plants. So what do you think? Do plants wish for baby plants?

Michael: It's a nice idea.

Dawn: I could write a poem about it.

Me: But do they really?

Richard: Well—sort of they do and sort of they don't.

Me: What are the respects in which they do, and what are the respects in which they don't?

Richard: That's hard.

The members of my class dutifully read out their assigned parts, and afterward we had a brief discussion. They followed up one or two loose ends left by the dialogue. For example, one student suggested that a plant's tendency to shrivel up its leaves when it needs water would not be an adaptive advantage in the way I had suggested if there were no creatures about to respond to this "message" by watering them. I agreed.

Perhaps I convinced a few members of my class that the question 'do plants have desires?' is somewhat more interesting than they had first thought. But I suspect that the effect of my pedagogical exercise was slight. I doubt that any of those alert, committed teachers and prospective teachers came to think, as a result of "perform-ing" my dialogue, that the concept of desire is a deeply problematic notion or that there may be formidable ob-stacles in the way of knowing what entities are capable of having "real" desires.

So here were two classroom discussions—one among twenty adults in Boston, Massachusetts, the other among seven schoolchildren in Edinburgh, Scotland. The dis-cussions had much in common. Each turned on a difficult mental concept—desire in the one case, happiness in the other. Each group expressed serious reservations about attributing a mental life to plants. Donald, in Edinburgh, spoke for both groups when he said at the beginning of our discussion of whether flowers can be happy, "You could say they are alive physically, but not mentally."

One difference between the two discussions was that the adults frequently appealed to a distinction between what is literally the case and what is only figuratively, or metaphorically, so. Thus a plant, the adults agreed, might be said metaphorically to want baby plants, but not lit-erally. No doubt they would also have said that flowers may be said metaphorically, but not literally, to be happy.

Appeal to the literal-figurative distinction might seem to mark a considerable intellectual advance. But in many cases—and this, I fear, is one—the appearance of ad-vance is largely illusory. The adults were not able to say what is required for an organism to be capable of having desires in a literal sense of 'desire,' let alone what makes it appropriate to say metaphorically that plants have de-sires. Without a clear understanding of the literal sense, as well as the grounds for metaphorical application, it really doesn't help much to say that it is only by a metaphor that a plant could be said to wish for baby plants.

The kids were able to use their imaginations more freely than the adults. Thus they came up with remarks like these:

"If you went bam! and hit them, they wouldn't start crying. They would get scratched and then start to die, probably."

"Inside a flower there is something that looks like an eye."

"Plants might be able to talk to each other by, you know, radio waves, or something like that, or by dust that goes from one plant to another."

The adults were prepared to concede some artistic and literary value to the use of the imagination. But they were not especially free with their own imaginations, and they insisted on keeping what they thought was a clear distinction between fact and fiction.

It's certainly true that to know whether plants have desires or can be happy, one needs to know as much as possible about the actual, as opposed to the merely fanciful, life of plants. But one also needs to think about possibilities. Suppose a plant could talk, or see, or move deliberately. Would that show that it sometimes wants to say or do something? And what would prove that the language was real, or that the plant was actually seeing something, or really acting deliberately?

By considering whether, if something *could* do this or that, it *would* have a desire (or be happy), we can hope to get clearer about what desires are, and what happiness is, and hence what it is to have desires or be happy. Only if we are clear about what it is to have a desire, or be happy, will we be able to grasp the fact, if it is one, that no plant has a desire or is happy. Thus the adult insistence that teachers and parents make clear to children that plants don't, in a literal sense, have desires, is really misplaced. Without the free exploration of possibilities, one will remain unclear about what it is to have a desire, and hence one will not be able to assess the facts or form a reasonable judgment as to whether plants do have desires. One may mouth the words, but without understanding.

Stories

WHEN I FIRST BEGAN meeting with the Juniors of St. Mary's, I told them what I wanted to do with them, and I read some examples of stories that raise interesting questions we could discuss together. The first story I read began this way:

Frog and Toad
were reading a book together.
"The people in this book are brave," said Toad.
"They fight dragons and giants
and they are never afraid."
"I wonder if we are brave,"
said Frog.
Frog and Toad looked into a mirror.
"We look brave," said Frog.
"Yes, but are we?"
asked Toad.[1]

1. Arnold Lobel, *Frog and Toad Together* (New York: Harper and Row, 1972), pp. 42–43.

In the manner of the heroes of myth and saga, Frog and Toad then undertake a perilous journey. Though the story is called "Dragons and Giants," Frog and Toad don't slay any dragons or face down any giants. Instead they meet perils that might be considered archetypal for their species. First a snake emerges from a cave with the words, "Hello, lunch." Frog and Toad manage to avoid becoming lunch for him. Then an avalanche threatens to flatten them both. Again, they manage somehow to survive. Finally, the shadow of a hawk falls over them just in time to send them scurrying for shelter under a rock.

Each time Frog and Toad escape a peril, they tremble and chant, "We are not afraid!" When they finally reach the protection of Toad's house, Toad jumps into bed and pulls the covers over himself. Frog rushes into a cupboard and closes the door. They stay there for a long time, we are told, "just feeling very brave together" (p. 51).

Lobel's delightfully whimsical tale goads us, through its provocative humor, to reflect on what bravery is. Can one see whether someone is brave? How can I tell whether I myself am brave? Frog and Toad look in a mirror. Frog reports that they *look* brave (though he doesn't explain what looking brave looks like). "Yes," agrees Toad, "but are we?"

Does one need to face danger to prove one's bravery? Does one need to face danger to *be* brave? And what sort of danger? Does it have to be a traditional danger, one that is standard for the exercise of bravery? Suppose the danger is overwhelming or the mission is not worth the risk? May one hide or run away without sacrificing one's claim to bravery? Is it sometimes foolhardy to stand one's ground?

And what about trembling? Or even feeling scared? Do these cast doubt on a claim to bravery or even nullify it? Or is the very opposite true? Is fear essential to real bravery?

Among the children in my class at St. Mary's, "Dragons and Giants" was an instant success. I suggested that the story raised a question about what bravery is, and we talked a little about how it did this. Then I asked the children to tell me what is required for someone to be brave.

They told me that to be brave one must do something that is (1) dangerous but (2) not stupid. I suggested that someone who did something stupidly dangerous might be said to be "foolhardy." They seemed not to have the word, though they had the idea.

The deed required for bravery, they went on, must be performed (3) for an important reason and (4) not for a reward, though (5) a reward might result. Finally, they were all agreed that (6) whether one is scared or not is simply irrelevant to the question of bravery.

These six points flowed from the children with little encouragement from me. I supplied one or two examples to sharpen their intuitions, but mostly the ideas came directly without special prodding.

In asking what is *required* for bravery, I was asking what conditions are *necessary* for being brave. But sometimes I asked whether someone who did this or that would, for that reason alone, have to count as being brave. Then I was asking for *sufficient* conditions for being brave. A satisfactory analysis of bravery would account for both what is necessary and what is sufficient for bravery.

The six points that the children came up with are, I think, neither necessary nor sufficient. Hence they do not constitute a complete analysis of bravery. As for necessity, one can, I think, be brave without actually doing anything dangerous if, say, one agrees to undertake a dangerous mission that never materializes, or if one does something one mistakenly thinks is dangerous. Then there is the bravery of facing ridicule, which is not allowed for in the children's analysis. Again, there may be bravery in facing death from a dread disease, though this is not really a matter of doing anything dangerous.

The six points are also not sufficient for bravery, I think. For example, a person who did something very dangerous in complete ignorance of the danger involved would not thereby be brave. But even though the six points are neither necessary nor sufficient for bravery, they offer a better analysis of bravery than anything one can find in Plato. No doubt they are inferior to the sophisticated account of bravery in Aristotle's *Nicomachean Ethics*, but I'm sure Aristotle spent much longer on his analysis than these children did on theirs.

From a very young age our children are admonished to be brave. Yet the notion of bravery is an extremely difficult one to be clear about. I could say that we ought to help our children think about the concept of bravery; but I suspect that most adults, if they are prepared to think freshly with children about what is required for bravery, will learn quite as much from the exercise as the children do. So I will say instead that we and our children ought to help each other think about the concept of bravery and what it is to be brave.

The second week I brought along a rather different example to my class, a selection from *Ozma of Oz* by L. Frank Baum. I read to the children the passage in which Dorothy and her companion, the talking hen Billina, come upon the mechanical man, Tiktok, in a rock vault. Printed on a card that hung from Tiktok's back were these instructions:

> For THINKING:—Wind the Clock-work Man under his left arm, (marked No. 1.)
> For SPEAKING:—Wind the Clock-work Man under his right arm, (marked No. 2.)
> For WALKING and ACTION:—Wind Clock-work in the middle of the back, (marked No. 3.)[2]

Dorothy read the directions out to Billina.

> "Well, I declare!" gasped the yellow hen, in amazement; "if the copper man can do half of these things he is a wonderful machine. But I suppose it is all humbug, like so many other patented articles."
> "We might wind him up," suggested Dorothy, "and see what he'll do." . . .
> "Which shall I wind up first?" she asked, looking again at the directions on the card.
> "Number One, I should think," returned Billina. "That makes him think, doesn't it?"
> "Yes," said Dorothy, and wound up Number One, under the left arm.
> "He doesn't seem any different," remarked the hen, critically.

2. L. Frank Baum, *Ozma of Oz* (Chicago: Rand McNally, 1907), p. 44.

"Why, of course not; he is only thinking, now," said Dorothy.

"I wonder what he is thinking about."

"I'll wind up his talk, and then perhaps he can tell us," said the girl.

So she wound up Number Two, and immediately the clock-work man said, without moving any part of his body except his lips:

"Good morn-ing, lit-tle girl. Good morn-ing, Mrs. Hen."

The words sounded a little hoarse and creaky, and they were uttered all in the same tone, without any change of expression whatever; but both Dorothy and Billina understood them perfectly.[3]

After I had finished reading the chapter, which continues for another two and a half pages, we talked about it.

"Could something that is not alive speak?" I asked the children.

"Yes," they said, giving the example of a talking doll. Then they became less sure. Several expressed reservations.

"The doll doesn't really speak," said Esther. "Someone spoke and made a recording. That gets played when you pull the string."

"It just says what's on the tape, whatever is happening," said David-Paul, "but Tiktok said, 'Good morning, Mrs. Hen,' when there was a hen there."

I went on to ask whether something that was not alive could think. Again, it was David-Paul who responded.

---

3. Ibid., pp. 44–46.

"A computer can reach down and get something out of its memory bank," he said. "That's like thinking. But a computer isn't alive." A little later in the discussion he said, "Maybe somebody could take a brain from someone who had died and put it in a machine—like Tiktok. And it would then have memory and could think, though it couldn't be alive."

"Why wouldn't it be alive?" I asked.

"Because," he said, "it wouldn't have a heart pumping blood; maybe it could have a pump pumping petrol [gasoline] through the brain instead."

The children's responses to these two stories reassured me that they would know how to think about questions that a story raises. So I began the practice of bringing along the beginning of a story that I wanted them to help me finish. They quickly caught on to the idea of discussing whatever issue my story-beginning raised. The next week they would try to find the points they had made in my continuation of the story.

In using this strategy to provoke dialogue I had at least two rather different aims in mind. One was to give them the idea that the conclusion we reached, if any, depended heavily, if not exclusively, on them. In fact I sometimes invented a story conclusion (as in "The Flower Question") just to bring about some sort of resolution. Moreover, I sometimes injected into the story-continuation questions or comments that hadn't actually come up in the first discussion. I did this if I thought the discussion hadn't been as searching as it should have been, or if we had overlooked some central point. But I tried to frame my conclusions with full respect for the integrity of the children's contributions. And I always tried to incorporate as much as I could of what the children had actually said. I thought it was important for them to have the sense that what they said mattered, that it would, so to speak, go into the record.

My other main aim was to encourage them to accept the problems as something they might want to think through for themselves. I didn't want them saying to me at the end of a period, "Well, now, what is the answer?"—as if I, but not they, were allowed to see the answers "at the back of the book." In fact I never got that response. They quickly claimed the problems as their own and took responsibility for dealing with them as best they could.

Cheese

THE FIRST ANECDOTE I gave my adult class in Boston, the year before my stay in Edinburgh, was this one:

Maxine: You know, cheese is made of grass.
Teacher: Why do you say that?
Maxine: Because cheese is made of milk, and cows give milk and cows eat grass.
Teacher: Do you eat cheese?
Maxine: Yeah.
Teacher: Then are you made of grass, too?
Maxine: No, I'm a human.

This exchange is part of a somewhat longer conversation between a teacher and an eight-year-old child that was passed on to me by someone in the School of Education at the University of Massachusetts in Amherst.[1] I shortened the exchange, supplied the name 'Maxine,' and asked half my adult class to write short papers in which they would continue the conversation with Maxine.

Some of the papers I received in response were solemn and didactic, some showed a good sense of fun. Some were rather formal, others were free and imaginative. (In fact, despite my somewhat peevish comments in the chapter before last, this class was a joy to teach.)

Most of the paper writers picked up the idea that Maxine thought human beings stand apart from the animal world. Some wanted Maxine to realize that we share with beasts an animal nature—that we are, after all, human *animals*. Others wanted to explore with her what is special and distinctive about human beings—what we *don't* share with beasts.

Whatever line these adults took on the last part of the Maxine fragment, however, they were in almost unanimous agreement that Maxine's first statements display a logical howler. Some said they wished they could explain the mistake to her but didn't know how to proceed. One expressed the hope that taking my course might prepare her to diagnose and correct Maxine's mistake. Others thought they knew what the mistake was, though in fact they were not successful in identifying a mistake.

Some members of my class thought that according to Maxine, if x eats y, then unless x is a human being, x is made of y. This is the principle that unless you are a human being, you are what you eat. The trouble with

1. It is recorded in Frank Self, "The Use of Food in Early Childhood Learning," Ph.D. dissertation, University of Massachusetts, 1979, pp. 183–184.

this as the basis for reconstructing Maxine's reasoning is that Maxine never says that cows are made of grass. It's *cheese* that she says is made of grass. And her reason for saying so is that cheese is made of milk, and cows give milk and cows eat grass. Thus we have these four statements:

(1) Cows eat grass.

(2) Cows give milk.

(3) Cheese is made of milk.

(4) Cheese is made of grass.

Why should anyone think that the last statement, 'Cheese is made of grass,' follows from the others? The obvious answer, it seems to me, is that the first two statements are thought to support an intermediate conclusion,

(2.5) Milk is made of grass,

and that, together with (3), 'Cheese is made of milk,' yields, by a principle of transitivity,

(4) Cheese is made of grass.

Thus: Milk is made of grass; cheese is made of milk; therefore cheese is made of grass.

Is the made-of relation really transitive? I'm inclined to think so. If it is, Maxine's inference is a good one. Now what about the first inference, the one from

(1) Cows eat grass

and

(2) Milk comes from cows

to

(2.5) Milk is made of grass. (?)

That inference is certainly much more questionable, but it's not entirely wild. By using a little imagination, we can see that it, too, has considerable plausibility. One needs to have the idea that the cow is, so to speak, a milk-producing machine. The cow eats grass, processes it in her belly, and turns it into the product, milk. In fact, further questioning of the child I have called "Maxine" showed that such was, in fact, the child's idea. (Teacher: "Why isn't cheese green?" Child: "When the cows eat grass it goes into their stomach and then gets changed around and comes out milk. The milk is made in the cow's stomach." What a neat and plausible account of what goes on in the bellies of cows!)

Some people insist that no child under the age of eight (as Maxine was) can understand or use a transitivity principle, such as the principle that if A is made of B and B is made of C, then A is made of C. Among developmental psychologists this is a point of controversy. I asked my Boston class if they were reluctant to attribute such reasoning to Maxine because of her young age. They said no, though perhaps with some hesitation. So why did they think there *must* be a mistake in her reasoning?

I think the explanation is this. The *idea* of developmental psychology has had a greater influence on the way adults think about children than have any specific findings of developmental psychologists, or any specific theories as to how children develop. Adults who have very little notion of what a child of age so-and-so is supposed to be capable of thinking accept the idea that children's thinking goes through various stages and that, roughly speaking, the changes from stage to stage are changes from relative inadequacy to relative adequacy. Maxine can thus be expected to suffer from various limitations in either her repertory of concepts or her ability to reason or, of course, both. If she says something strange, something really peculiar or unusual, something that seems not to be the result of simple ignorance or misinformation, it must be, one naturally assumes, that her idea is the result of some conceptual limitation or some limitation in her ability to reason or both.

One unfortunate result of this is that it predisposes one to ignore, or misunderstand, the really imaginative and inventive thinking of young children. If one is predisposed to rack up "oddball" questions and unpalatable conclusions to cognitive incompetence, one will miss much that is interesting in what children have to say to us.

The "Maxine" exchange seemed a natural one to try out on my Juniors at St. Mary's, all of whom were older than Maxine. But being innocent of the assumptions of developmental psychology, they would be unlikely to take a condescending attitude toward the reasoning just because it sounded strange and came from the mouth of a child.

Here is the story-beginning I brought to class:

"Hello, Freddie, how was school?"

It was Freddie's mother, greeting him as he came up the garden path.

"Good," replied Freddie; "but you know, we've got this weird kid from Stornoway in my science class. He's called Ian. He whispered to me during class today, 'Cheese is made of grass.' 'You've got to be kidding,' I said. Then Mr. McColl, our teacher, noticed us talking and asked what it was all about. Ian repeated what he had said to me—'Cheese is made of grass.' 'That's a very interesting bit of reasoning.' Mr. McColl said, 'we must discuss it next week.' What do you suppose he meant?"

"That's easy," said Alice, who had been eating a yogurt in the doorway and listening in on the conversation. "He means that cows make milk out of grass and farmers make cheese out of milk. If *a* is made of *b* and *b* is made of *c*, then *a* is made of *c*. Cheese is made of milk and milk is made of grass, so cheese is made of grass."

By this time Freddie had made it into his front hallway and had dropped his books onto the floor. He gave Alice a dirty look. Then he turned to his mother. "Is Alice right, Mum?" he asked.

"Let's talk about it over the dinner table," replied his mother. "I have an errand to run just now."

My class at St. Mary's found Alice's reasoning quite acceptable.

"In a way it's true," said Donald.

"We don't really notice what stuff is actually made of," suggested Esther, who was especially intent on sharing what she knew about milk production in cows. "You know," she told us in amazement, "they have four different stomachs."

Donald seemed to sum things up for most of these children when he said, "It sounds unusual, but grass *is* cheese, in a way; it's just the first stage of what becomes cheese—the second stage is milk."

"Cream!" put in someone as a correction.

"The third stage is cheese," Donald continued. "It's

all the same thing really, it's just different stages as it matures."

After a while, though, we began discussing whether there is a difference between what something is made *from* and what it is made *of*. A book, they wanted to say, is made *of* paper. But paper, most agreed, is not really made *of* wood, though it may be made *from* wood. "If it was made *of* wood," suggested Martin, in what was surely the virtuoso remark of that whole discussion, "it would be, you know, *wooden*." (Martin was then almost exactly ten.)

So in the end my kids in Edinburgh withdrew their endorsement of Maxine's reasoning. They were willing to say that milk is made by cows *from* grass, and that cheese is made by farmers *from* milk or, perhaps, from cream. But they were inclined to deny, correctly, I should say, though they didn't ask my opinion, that cheese is made *of* milk and also to deny that milk is made *of* grass.

Here is the way I used the children's insight in the conclusion of the story:

> Alice didn't come to dinner that evening. She had an early snack and then went off with a friend to see a film. But Auntie Gertie came. She was better to talk to about difficult things anyway, thought Freddie. Of course Alice didn't agree. She considered Aunt Gertie simple-minded and sentimental.
>
> "What was that you wanted to talk about, Freddie?" began Freddie's mother as she served the tuna-fish casserole. "Was it something about a school chum saying cheese is made of rope?"
>
> "Not rope, Mother, *grass*," said Freddie impatiently; "and he's not a chum of mine. He's a strange

kid from Stornoway who likes to talk Gaelic, and even when he speaks English, he says strange things."

"Why would anyone say cheese is made of grass?" asked Freddie's father, "unless . . ." he paused, "unless, of course, he thought the specks of blue in blue cheese were bits of grass."

"No, Dad, that's not it at all," said Freddie. "What he meant . . . I think, at least this was Alice's idea, is that people make cheese out of milk, or cream, maybe, and cows make milk or cream out of grass. So, if one kind of stuff is made of another and the other is made of some third kind of stuff, then the first is made of the third. So cheese is made of grass. Do you think that's right, Auntie Gertie?"

Aunt Gertie pushed her peas onto her fork thoughtfully. "It *is* interesting reasoning," she replied slowly, "yet it does leave us a little unhappy with the conclusion." She thought a bit more. "Maybe," she went on, "we need to distinguish between what things are made *of* and what they are made *from*."

"What do you mean?" asked Freddie, who was now more puzzled than ever.

"Well, let's take an example," said Aunt Gertie. "Wine is made *from* grape juice, and vinegar is made *from* wine. But vinegar isn't really made *of* wine, let alone grape juice. You could say that vinegar is the last stage in a long process."

"Oh, I think I get it," said Freddie, "and paper is made *from* wood, not *of* wood. If it was made *of* wood it would be . . . wooden, like a wooden house or a wooden table."

"Excellent!" said Aunt Gertie.

"And so," Freddie rushed on, "Alice wasn't right after all. Smart old Alice tripped up this time. Because cheese isn't made *of* milk, it's made *from* it. And milk isn't made *of* grass, it's made *from* it. If milk was made *of* grass, it would be . . . it would be *grassy*. Yuk!"

"Don't be too hard on Alice," said Aunt Gertie. "She did a good job of explaining what the boy from Stornoway probably meant. Most people don't think much about the difference between what something is made of and what it's made from."

"Still, she did goof," insisted Freddie triumphantly. "Smart old Alice goofed." He was barely able to wait until he had a chance to point out to her the distinction she had overlooked. "When will Alice be back from the cinema?" he asked eagerly.

The Ship

SHORTLY AFTER MY WIFE, my son, and I arrived in Edinburgh in August of 1982, we learned that two square-rigged sailing vessels would be visiting the nearby port of Leith. Because we all like sailing ships, we took a bus to Leith on one of the days appointed for visiting, and we looked the ships over. They were lovely to see, even close at hand with their sails hauled in and their cabins open to close scrutiny.

The guide, who gave us a little lecture on the history of these two ships and on the nature of the voyage they were currently taking around Britain, made several comments about one of the ships that astonished and amused my wife and son. The *Ciudad de Inca* had been built, he said, in 1846, but had been sunk shortly thereafter in a great battle. She had been raised in 1981 and restored in a complicated process that involved eventually replacing some 85 percent of her timbers. But it had all been worthwhile, he said, for now she was probably the oldest square-rigged sailing ship afloat.

My wife and son couldn't believe their ears. They were all too familiar with philosophers' puzzles about identity through time. The most famous of these puzzles has to do with the fabled ancient ship of Theseus, each of whose boards was replaced one at a time until all the boards were new. The puzzle is to say at what point (and why exactly then!) the old ship ceased to exist. My family couldn't believe that this guide would happily conjoin, without the slightest sign of puzzlement or embarrassment, the claims that (1) over 85 percent of the ship's boards were new and (2) she was perhaps the oldest square-rigger afloat.

Two months later, when I began getting my St. Mary's class to help me finish stories, I naturally thought of this episode and made it the basis for a story I brought into class for completion. Here is the crucial part of what I gave the children to reflect on:

At the dinner table that evening Freddie was asked to tell his family what he and Angus had seen in Leith Harbor. He was still very excited, but not too excited to tell them about the tall masts, the endless rigging, the cozy cabins, the small bunks where the crew slept and, of course, the double-decker bus where you buy tickets to board the ship.

"It's a very beautiful ship," Freddie explained. "It's all gleaming white. It's like a ship in a movie. In fact, it has been used in making pirate films."

"How old did you say the ship is?" asked Freddie's father.

"I think the guide said it was built about 1840 or something," replied Freddie, "but only a few years later it got sunk in a big battle. It stayed on the ocean bottom for years and years. Then about two years ago it was salvaged, brought up from the bottom. It's now the oldest sailing ship afloat."

"Really!" put in Freddie's mother. "Then it must be quite dilapidated."

"Oh, no!" Freddie assured her, "not at all. The guide told us that when they brought it up . . . uh, brought *her* up . . ."—Freddie suddenly remembered that ships are considered feminine—"they found that much of the decking was rotten. So they replaced most of that, board by board. Then they found that some of the ribs were rotten too, so they replaced them. Finally, they got worried about the sides, you know, the outside of the hull. They ended up replacing much of that as well, one board at a time. Now almost all the boards on the ship are new, and very smooth and solid and well painted. She's a beautiful ship."

"Then it can't be the oldest sailing ship afloat," sneered Alice, ignoring the rule about calling ships "her." "It can't be, if almost all the boards are new. It's a new ship. It may be modeled after an old ship, but it's a new ship."

Freddie was stunned. He had been imagining the battles the *Maria Magdalena* had fought. He had been wondering what the sailors who had sailed her were like and what it would have been like to be a cabin boy on the ship when she had set sail for the Far East. He had been so proud to be standing on the deck of a ship that had sailed so long ago.

Now it seemed to Freddie that Alice was right. The ship he and Angus had boarded in Leith Harbor, the ship the guide had said was the oldest

sailing ship afloat, wasn't really; she was only a copy
of the *Maria Magdalena*. No, she wasn't exactly a
copy either. She was something the *Maria Magdalena* had . . . sort of . . . turned into . . . a new ship
the old ship had turned into.

But the guide had said she was the oldest square-
rigger afloat. Freddie was sure of that.

As we read the story-beginning together the kids began
to get interested in the issues raised. But before we
launched into a full-scale discussion, I checked to make
sure they understood the problem.

"What's the problem?" I asked.

"The problem is that . . . we want to find out which
is which," Donald replied. "Is the ship the old ship, or
is the ship just a model, a replica, a copy of the original
ship?"

David-Paul seemed not to be puzzled. "That's easy,"
he said.

Me: "Why is it easy?"

David-Paul: "If there are still a few planks left, it's
the old ship."

Esther: "There must be some planks left."

David-Paul: "Perhaps the spirit of the old ship would
still be there. It's not really a new ship if it's still got
some of the old timbers . . . and the spirit of the old
ship."

I wanted to follow up the idea that whether it is still
the old ship might depend on whether the "spirit" of
the old ship is present. But the discussion moved too
fast for me to work in an appropriate question. In fact,
very soon after he mentioned the idea of the "spirit" of
the old ship, David-Paul changed his attitude radically;

he changed from a rather permissive stand on what is required for persistence to a much stricter, or perhaps more skeptical, point of view. Then it was too late to sound him out on the idea of a ship's spirit.

But I'm jumping ahead. First there was a rather heated discussion of several textual points (for example, how many boards would have to be replaced for "almost all" to be replaced?) and some other preliminary remarks. I sought to refocus the problem.

Me: "Suppose there is a little of the old decking left that has never been replaced. Everything in the middle has been replaced. And suppose it has the old keel. And everything else has been replaced. The masts are new, the sails are new. How many would say it is the old ship?"

All hands went up. By this time I had sketched the ship on the board.

Me: "Suppose we replaced those last boards. Suppose the captain came along one day and said those boards are rotten, too. And they replaced them. Suppose the only thing left from the old ship is the keel. How many say it is still the old ship?"

Again all hands went up.

Me: "So the keel is the important thing?"

David-Paul: "I think the ribs and the keel are the most important parts of it."

I persisted, "But so long as the keel remains, it's the same ship?"

David-Paul: "No. People never see the keel anyway."

Donald: "It doesn't matter whether you can see it. That doesn't mean it isn't the old ship, just because people can't see that it is."

Donald's point was extremely well taken. We wanted

to know whether it would *be* the old ship under these imaginable conditions or those. We were not asking whether people would *recognize* it as the old ship.

Yet David-Paul had a point, too. What counts as being the old ship is partly a question of the criteria people use to determine whether the ship has persisted through this change or that. If no one ever checked on the keel, it would be irrelevant.

Ise: "[Suppose] it's still got the old cabin on it."

Donald: "It doesn't matter whether you build something new onto it, as long as it's the same ship underneath."

Of course, to say, "It's still got the old cabin on it," is not really to commit oneself to there being a ship quite independent of the cabin. I can say of a chair, "It's still got its back on it," without committing myself to the view that something can continue to be a chair even without a back rather than, say, becoming a stool. Still, Donald's comment was on target. If we think of the cabin as something *on* the ship, as a sort of accessory, then the fact that the cabin has persisted does not settle anything about whether the ship itself has.

By this time in the discussion David-Paul had rethought the matter and had begun to assume something of the role of a prosecuting attorney. He took upon himself the task of exposing what now seemed to him to be the flimsiness of the class's prevailing, rather permissive attitude. Donald became the spokesman for this dominant view. The ensuing discussion was especially impressive for the naturalness with which the protagonists reached for analogies to support their positions. I often admonish my university students (and myself!) to think of relevant analogies. These children exploited analogies brilliantly without any outside encouragement.

David-Paul chose the analogy of a castle. That isn't surprising, in a way, since the landscape around him was dominated by Edinburgh Castle. Nevertheless, the choice was extraordinarily apt.

"So *they* mean to say," he said, with an emphasis on 'they' and a tone of voice that suggested he was confident he could commit the others, the permissive ones, to an analogy they would soon be uncomfortable with, "that if you've got this castle that's completely rebuilt and that's only got this one stone from the old castle—all the other stones are new—that it's the old castle."

Several of the others replied, "No," though most of them did not immediately see how to avoid being committed to the unwanted analogy.

Donald chose the analogy of a car, an analogy he returned to several times in the discussion. "So, I've got a car," he said. "I replace a window, another window. I replace a door, all the doors, wheels . . . it's the same car as long as I don't replace the engine."

We considered whether there might be some part of the ship, the persistence of which would count as heavily in determining whether the ship persists as the engine counts in determining whether the car persists. No one could come up with a good candidate, other than perhaps the keel. To test the importance of the keel, I changed the thought experiment. "Suppose," I said, "we decide that if the keel stays the same, it's the same ship. I want you to imagine another situation. We have this old ship and we replace only one thing, and that's the keel. Everything else stays the same."

Donald: "Oh that would still be exactly the same ship. Still the old ship. Definitely."

Me: "So why is the keel so important?"

Donald: "It's not necessarily that the keel is the most important. You could do that with any piece . . . I could say, 'I know what I'll do; I'll take one of these masts away and put a new one in.' It would still be the same ship. It's not necessarily that the keel is special. It's just that the keel is the one that . . . It's hard to explain . . ."

At this point David-Paul moved in with his most effective investigative skills. "You mean to say, Donald," he asked, "that if there was only one little piece of wood left"—he gestured to indicate a very small piece—"that would still be the same ship? . . . If there's just one little piece of wood left and the rest is all new, would that still be an old ship?"

Donald: "But still, that means that the rest of the bits that replace [the others] would be built onto this little piece to make it still the same ship."

Here and elsewhere in the discussion Donald made clear his appreciation for the importance of continuity in this matter. So long as the changes are gradual, if we start out with *Maria Magdalena*, and at every point in the evolution there is a ship present, then so long as some bit of the original remains at the end, the most appropriate answer to the question 'What ship do we have now?' will be 'Maria Magdalena.'

As it happened, the newspapers and television in Britain at that time were full of stories about efforts to salvage the Tudor vessel *Mary Rose*. "If you dig up something like the *Mary Rose*," Donald said at one point, "and you find something like the rib cage, and this is too rotten, and that is too rotten, and there is still one bit that doesn't need to be replaced, and you say, 'we'll keep this bit here,' and you build up the ship around it . . ."

David-Paul was unimpressed. "You're saying," he said contemptuously, "if one grain, one splinter, survives, and they build the whole ship around it, that's the oldest ship."

Donald: "No. If they had the original ship and they said, "Oh dear! Look at this ship here! It's all gone rotting . . .""

Donald seemed to be trying hard to distinguish the case in which someone simply takes a piece from an old ship or castle and builds around it a new ship or castle, from the case in which gradual changes are made in a decayed and rotten ship or castle.

David-Paul wanted to know exactly how much of the original ship would have to remain for the ship to persist. Suppose, he suggested, there was just a splinter left.

Donald: "If it was a splinter, that would be different. You've got to agree, that would be going a bit too far."

David-Paul: "Okay, a block of wood *that* big, then." He gestured to mark off a block of wood the size of a large book.

Donald hesitated. "Okay," he said, "that's also going a bit too far . . ."

Later Donald seemed to think he could live with the conclusion that the ship with only a substantial block left from the original material was still the old ship. But he insisted, with even greater emphasis, that there must be continuity and only gradual replacement. "If you take these bits off and replace them," he said, "and then take all these bits and replace them"—he was gesturing all the while—"it would still be the same ship."

David-Paul was contemptuous. He made as if to point

to the surviving block. "But that's the *old* part of the ship," he said. "The rest is all new, 1982."

Donald: "It's still an old ship."

David-Paul: "Yeah, that *bit* of the ship."

Donald: "Yeah, but it would still be an old ship."

David-Paul: "The best thing to do is to take that piece of wood and drop it in the water and make it float around"—mockingly—"the oldest ship."

The excitement of that discussion is hard to describe. Everything flowed naturally, yet the analogies, the rhetorical flourishes, and the sudden insights burst on us like a fireworks display.

I had no trouble writing a continuation to the story, using the material in that wonderful discussion. But I backed away from contriving a resolution of the debate between Donald and David-Paul. Donald had begun to come up with a plausible criterion of persistence for bodies like ships; he seemed prepared to live with the unintuitive consequences of his emerging criterion—that, for example, the ship might be *Maria Magdalena* all right, even though the only material left from what was used to build *Maria Magdalena* was a small block of wood.

David-Paul had assumed, very effectively, a critical and skeptical stance, but he had not begun to formulate a criterion that might be compared to Donald's. Nor had he explored the consequences of living with a basically skeptical position. I made some tentative efforts the following week to push the investigation further, but then I decided we would need a completely fresh start to make any significant progress. I thought we might return to the issues later in the year, perhaps with a consideration of the persistence of human bodies, or even the persistence of human persons, but in fact we never did.

Here is the way I made the story end:

"How do we know whether she has the spirit of the old ship?" asked Freddie skeptically. "And what's so special about the keel? You don't even see the keel; it's under water."

"Well," answered Angus, "whether you can see it doesn't matter. She could be the old ship even if we couldn't see that she is. But I guess I agree, the keel isn't really so special. It's just that *some* boards remain and the others were replaced one at a time. So there was always a ship there. You couldn't just take a piece from the *Maria Magdalena* and build a ship around it and have an old ship—any more than you could take a stone from Edinburgh Castle and build a castle around it with new stones and call what you had built an old castle."

"I see," said Freddie, getting very excited again, "if you've got an old ship, you don't destroy her by replacing one of her boards. You've still got a ship, and it must be the old one you've got, though she's a little different now."

"We're not worried about one board," agreed Angus. "That's no problem."

"Then," Freddie went on, getting more and more excited, "you replace another board. You've changed her a tiny bit more, but she's still the old ship. She'll go on being the old ship, just getting new boards, unless, of course, you finally replace *all* the old boards."

"Wait a minute," said Angus; it was his turn to be skeptical. "Suppose you just have one tiny piece left that belonged to the ship at the beginning—a tiny, tiny piece, maybe just a splinter—everything else new, 1982. How could it still be the old ship?"

"That would be going too far," agreed Freddie, "if there was just a splinter."

"Well, suppose it was bigger than a splinter, but just one small piece of board," suggested Angus.

Freddie hesitated. "I guess that would still be going too far," he admitted.

"But how far is too far?" pressed Angus, "and how far can you go without going too far? One *big* board? Would that be enough to make the whole ship the *Maria Magdalena?*"

"I don't know," said Freddie, exhausted with all the hard thinking he had been doing. "I'm tired. Let's see what's on the telly."

Knowledge

I RECENTLY came across an account of a very unusual kindergarten class. The teacher was so interested in the discussions of her class and so anxious to follow up those discussions that she tape-recorded and transcribed them later the same day—before the conversations had faded in her memory and in time to think about a follow-up the next day, if that should be called for. The book contains many extended excerpts from those discussions. They are wonderful. The kids are imaginative, playful, inventive, and remarkably free. The freshness of the discussions is a profound tribute to the teacher who made them possible.

Consider this exchange, which takes place after the class has planted lettuce seeds:

Eddie: . . . how do we know it's really lettuce?
Teacher: The label says "Bibb Lettuce."
Eddie: What if it's really tomatoes?

Teacher: Oh. Are you wondering about the picture of tomatoes with the lettuce on the packet? It's just an idea for salad, after the lettuce comes up.

Warren: They might think they're lettuce seeds and they might not know.

Earl: Maybe the seeds look the same as something else.

Teacher: Do you think they could make such a mistake?

Lisa: Just bring it back to the store if it's wrong.

Deana: The store people didn't even make it.

Eddie: You have to take it back to the gardener.

Deana: Maybe they printed a word they wanted to spell the wrong way. Maybe they mixed it up.

Eddie: They could have meant to put different seeds in there and then they turned around and went to the wrong table.

Wally: The wrong part of the garden. The tomato part.

Warren: So in case it's not lettuce it could be tomatoes.[1]

Eddie's question is about evidence and the warrant for knowledge. The other children join in immediately; they happily think of various possibilities that tend to undermine the justification we might have thought we had for believing that those seeds are indeed lettuce seeds. In this way they call into question the claim to knowledge.

Anyone who has taken a course in philosophy will be

1. Paley, *Wally's Stories*, pp. 183–184.

familiar with the idea of raising questions that tend to undermine our claim to know such things as that the seeds in "that packet over there" are lettuce seeds. Once doubts have been raised, is there any way to dismiss them, rationally and responsibly? Is there perhaps some conceivable evidence that, if we had it, would give us an unshakable claim to know that those little things are indeed lettuce seeds? Or is the search for such evidence futile? After all, the label might be a mistake, the gardener might have misremembered, even an expert horticulturalist might make a mistake. Should we then conclude that nobody ever really *knows* that certain things are lettuce seeds? Of course we could always plant them, which is what the kindergarten children were doing. But the seeds might fail to germinate. A failure to germinate wouldn't establish that they weren't lettuce seeds. Even if they did germinate, there might be a problem in identifying the resulting plants. But aside from that, the most we could learn is that those seeds *were* lettuce seeds, or perhaps *were* not lettuce seeds. We might still wonder whether anybody ever knows whether certain things *are* lettuce seeds.

My family recently had a visitor, someone who had grown up and spent most of her life in cities. We planned a picnic, and our visitor was pleased. But when we suggested taking berry boxes along on the picnic so that we could pick wild blueberries, our visitor was alarmed. "How will I know they are edible?" she wanted to know. "That's easy," we said, "we'll tell you." Our visitor was not reassured. "You'll put me in the awkward position," she said, "of having to choose between offending you [by refusing to eat what you tell me is edible] and accepting

something I have insufficient evidence for." We reflected. "But how do you know to believe the labels on
the berries you buy in the store?" I asked, pleased with
my response. Her reply was quick. "I've had lots of
experience eating those," she said, smiling at herself.

As you can tell, I would like to join the discussion
with the class about seeds. I would like to puzzle out
with those kids whether we know and if so how we know
that certain little seeds are lettuce seeds. I was therefore
quite disappointed that the teacher took her children to
be preoccupied with merely practical considerations. Surely
there is nothing practical about thinking of ways in which
it could turn out that seeds in a perfectly ordinary (or at
least *apparently* perfectly ordinary) lettuce-seed package
might fail to contain lettuce seeds, especially when the
matter at stake is whether we *know* (as contrasted with,
say, strongly believe) that these are lettuce seeds. Here
is the beginning of pure reflection, with nothing practical
in sight.

Why is it that parents and teachers, even the most
sensitive and well-meaning of them, so often fail to grasp
the moments of pure reflection in children's thinking or
to recognize them for what they are? Perhaps it is because
so much emphasis has been placed on the development
of children's abilities, especially their cognitive abilities,
that we automatically assume their thinking is primitive
and in need of being developed toward an adult norm.
What we take to be primitive, however, may actually be
more openly reflective than the adult norm we set as the
goal of education. By filtering the child's remarks through
our developmental assumptions we avoid having to take
seriously the philosophy in those remarks; in that way
we also avoid taking the child and the child's point of

view with either the seriousness or the playfulness they deserve.

I decided to ask my class at St. Mary's about whether we can know that certain seeds are lettuce seeds. I went to a hardware store on George Street and bought a packet of (as it said on the packet) lettuce seeds. My first idea was to ask the children whether we really knew that the seeds in the packet were lettuce seeds. Then I expanded on that idea a bit. I decided to go back and buy a second packet of seeds, preferably seeds that resembled those in the first packet but were identified as something quite different, then ask the children how we might know, or what would be required for knowing, that the seeds in one of the packets were really lettuce seeds.

Unfortunately the hardware store I went to did not have "see-through" packets. I couldn't tell by looking at the outside of the packets which seeds might resemble lettuce seeds. I asked my wife, who consulted a friend. On their considered advice I bought a packet of carrot seeds, then transferred the seeds from the two packets into two clear envelopes.

At that point I became even more ambitious. I decided to introduce the idea of something being a *sufficient condition* for something else. At the beginning of that week's class I spent a little time on that technical notion. I asked my kids to give me a sufficient condition for

(1) That person is my father.

With a little encouragement they came up with

(2) That person is a man and he is one of my parents,

which is, indeed, a sufficient condition for (1). Then I passed around the class the two plastic envelopes of seeds and asked the kids what they thought they were. There were various guesses, including, eventually, "lettuce seeds." I admitted that one packet did contain lettuce seeds and the other carrot seeds. But I told them that what I was most interested in was not whether they could guess which was which, but whether they could give me a sufficient condition for

(3) I know that these [the seeds in one of the two clear packets] are lettuce seeds.

To add a bit of drama to the project I asked the children to imagine a situation in which one's mother says, "go out to the garden and plant the lettuce seeds," but alas, one has already emptied out both the lettuce seeds and the carrot seeds from their respective packets, and one doesn't remember anymore which lot of seeds came from which packet.

Martin was very practical. "I'd just shove them both in one spot," he said, "and get half lettuce, half carrots next year."

"Okay," I said, "but now what would have to be true for you to *know* which is which?"

Martin: "What if it says on the packet?"

"Good," I said, "let's try that." I then put on the board the conditional statement that, as I had explained to them earlier, was to state a sufficient condition for the claim in question. This was the conditional:

(4) If it says on the packet "lettuce seeds," then I know these are lettuce seeds.

I underlined the antecedent of that conditional and reminded them that if the conditional as a whole were true, the antecedent would give a sufficient condition for the conclusion—'I know that these are lettuce seeds.'

At this point in the discussion the children seemed quite happy to believe that what appears on the label is correct; quite unlike the kids in the kindergarten class, no one in my class seemed at all skeptical about statement (4).

There were other suggestions for sufficient conditions. Martin repeated his idea that one could plant all the seeds and then wait until spring to see which ones came up lettuce. I suggested that Martin's procedure might give us a sufficient condition for 'I know that those *were* lettuce seeds' but not for 'I know that these *are* lettuce seeds.'

Suddenly David-Paul became animated. "You could sample some out," he said. "You could take two [seeds] of each [kind] and plant them and mark where you put them, and put them in a greenhouse so they'll grow quicker and watch which came out lettuce and then you'd know and you could plant the right ones."

The idea was ingenious. Knowing which seeds are lettuce seeds is, in a way, knowing which seeds have a certain potentiality. We might determine that by forcing a sample of each lot to realize their potentiality on a speeded-up schedule. After learning in this way which seeds *were* lettuce seeds, we would have a splendid basis for inferring which of the remaining seeds *are* lettuce seeds.

Esther was curious to know which plastic packet in the classroom in fact had the lettuce seeds in it. So we suspended the discussion of sufficient conditions for knowledge, and I let the children guess. About half got the answer right. (At least I think so!)

I then tried to bring the children back to considering what was on the board, namely, the conditional statement (4). I wanted to know, I said, whether "it says on the packet 'lettuce seeds' " is *really* sufficient for "I know that these are lettuce seeds."

Martin: "Well, they might have got the packet wrong . . ."

Esther: "It's not likely."

Martin: ". . . and it's really sunflower seeds."

There was some confusion as to whether we were thinking of the seeds as being in a sealed packet. I made that condition explicit.

(4*) If it says on the *sealed* packet "lettuce seeds,"
       then I know that these are lettuce seeds.

I asked whether everyone was happy with the conditional, as revised.

Chorus: "Yes."

Me: "Is anybody worried that 'it says on the sealed packet "lettuce seeds" ' is not sufficient?"

Chorus. "No-o-o."

Martin (persisting): "Well, you might plant them all and then find out next summer that you've got sunflowers all over the garden. You'd be disappointed."

David-Paul; "But sunflower seeds look different."

Martin: "You wouldn't know, if they were enclosed in the packet, though, would you?"

Esther: "But if you're an experienced gardener, you would tell the difference."

Martin: "Well, [suppose] you plant them and you get daffodils coming up or something."

Someone: "They're bulbs."

Martin remained skeptical. But the others didn't take naturally to his skepticism, so I let the matter drop for that day and we went on to a story.

The next week, though, I returned with the class to the question of a sufficient condition for knowledge. In transcribing their discussion from the previous week I had been struck by the persistence of Martin's skepticism and by the fact that we had failed to relate any of the antiskeptical responses of the others to our project of providing a sufficient condition for knowledge.

To prime the follow-up discussion I handed out xeroxes of this:

We were discussing whether
  if it says on the packet "lettuce seeds"
  then I know that these are lettuce seeds.
I asked whether anybody was worried that the *antecedent* of that conditional statement ("it says on the packet 'lettuce seeds'") might not be a *sufficient condition* for the *consequent* ("I know that these are lettuce seeds").
Chorus. No-o-o.
Martin: Well, you might plant them all and then find out next summer that you've got sunflowers all over the garden. You'd be disappointed.
David-Paul: But sunflower seeds look different.
Martin: You wouldn't know if they were enclosed in the packet, though, would you?
Esther: But if you're an experienced gardener you would tell the difference.

I suggested to the children that we really hadn't taken account of the possibilities Martin was suggesting. Everybody liked the idea that a fragment of their actual conversation from the previous week was printed on the sheet of paper before them. I think they thought it added significance to what we were doing together. They were certainly prepared to reconsider the question of a sufficient condition for knowledge.

David-Paul was now quite circumspect. "Well, you'd *more-or-less* know," he said carefully. "You wouldn't suspect anything."

I brought them back to the transcript. Martin had said, I pointed out, that there could be "lettuce seeds" written on the packet and yet sunflowers come up. David-Paul had replied, I went on, "Sunflower seeds look different." But what, I asked, has that to do with what we have on the board?

Daniel (reading from the board): "If it says 'lettuce seeds' on the packet, then I know these are lettuce seeds."

Ise: "They could have put tomato seeds in the packet."

The children were now becoming a bit more skeptical. I tried to bring them back to the project of stating a sufficient condition for knowledge.

Me: "But if you say, 'Sunflower seeds look different' . . ."

Daniel: "They do."

Me: "Okay, but now you should add to the antecedent, "If it says 'lettuce seeds' on the packet *and they don't look like sunflower seeds* . . ."

David-Paul: "But that's wrong; it could be tomato seeds."

Me: "Okay [writing on the board] *or like tomato seeds* . . ."

David-Paul: "Or apple-tree seeds."

Me [still writing on the board]: "*or apple-tree seeds.*"

Martin: "Or carrot seeds."

Me [writing]: *"or carrot seeds."*

I then tried to sum up. "If somebody says, 'Sunflower seeds look different' or 'Carrot seeds look different' or, what Esther said, 'If you're an expert, you can tell'—"

Martin: "Yeah, but you might not be an expert."

Me: "If those points are relevant, then you have to say, '*If* you're an expert, then you'll know,' or something like that."

David-Paul: "If you took a *very reliable make* . . ."

By this time Esther had become cautious. "Still," she said to David-Paul, *"they* could get something wrong."

David-Paul: "They could get one out of a hundred packets wrong."

Esther: *"You* could have the one out of the hundred packets, couldn't you?"

David-Paul: "Esther, you're just making it difficult."

[General laughter]

Esther then presented an idea for turning amateurs into experts. She suggested there could be a picture on the back of the packet showing the different kinds of seeds, so we could each match up the seeds with the right picture.

It was David-Paul's turn to be difficult. "But it couldn't show them all," he said. "What happens if you get pineapple seeds?"

[Laughter]

Martin decided to elaborate on Esther's suggestion. "It could be a see-through packet," he suggested, "so that you could see what seeds are in there; then you could check them against the chart."

David-Paul: "Yeah, but it would cost too much. Anyway, you're supposed to trust the people who are giving it to you."

David-Paul's point was certainly relevant. Philosophers tend to discuss analyses of knowledge in abstraction from social context. In "real life" it might be quite objectionable—perhaps just boorish or insensitive, but perhaps downright immoral—to require that a theoretically sufficient condition for knowledge be satisfied before one will allow that one knows whatever is in question. Moreover, it might be offensive or even immoral to say that one *didn't* know that the bridge was unsafe, or the food poisoned, when one had actually been told, even if by someone whose credentials could be questioned.

I must admit that I didn't stop to acknowledge David-Paul's point, except with a rather weak "Maybe so." Instead I pressed on. "Whenever you suggest some way of making sure," I said, "like asking an expert or checking a chart, then that should be added here [to the antecedent of our conditional . . . for example], 'If we checked a chart and found it on the chart, *then* we would know.' "

David-Paul: "But isn't this a bit silly, though. If you're buying a packet of lettuce seeds, you're not going to go through this whole procedure to make sure they aren't sunflower seeds."

Me: "Okay, maybe it is silly. But then maybe you should say, "We don't *really* know . . .""

David-Paul: "You never really *know*, but it's a good enough chance."

As I look back on the transcript of those two discussions I am rather surprised at the way I encouraged skepticism. (I don't usually do that—at least, I don't *think* I do.) The skepticism I encouraged rests on the old, yet ever new, idea that real knowledge is incorrigible; if I really know that those are lettuce seeds, then not only am I in fact not mistaken, I couldn't possibly be mistaken. Conversely, if I *could* possibly be mistaken, then I don't really know.

This "strong" conception of knowledge is at least as old as Plato (see his *Republic* 477E); but also as old as Plato is a weaker notion, namely the idea that knowledge is true belief that is justified by one's ability to give a sound account of why what one believes to be so is so. (See Plato's *Meno* at around 98A and his *Theaetetus* at 201D.) This weaker notion (knowledge as justified true belief) doesn't require infallibility, it just requires that in fact no error was made and that the belief was well grounded.

The history of that branch of philosophy known as "epistemology" (or "theory of knowledge") includes a persistent attempt across the centuries to state in a satisfactory way what would be both necessary and sufficient conditions for knowledge on the weaker conception. When I talk with university students about the analysis of what knowledge is, I usually try to awaken in them the inclination to insist on the strong notion—to insist that is, that there is no real knowledge where there is even the possibility of being mistaken. But after I have awakened in them this inclination, I usually point out that according to the strong conception of knowledge, we don't know very much. I then go on to interest them in trying to state necessary and sufficient conditions for knowledge on the weaker conception.

I suppose the reason I didn't proceed in this way with my St. Mary's class was that I found them, to my surprise, rather less inclined to insist on incorrigibility than I had expected. Certainly Martin's skepticism did depend for its force on (1) distinguishing "real knowledge" from what David-Paul called "more-or-less knowing," and on (2) being inclined to suppose that "real knowledge" is limited to what (if anything!) one couldn't possibly be mistaken about. But the other children seemed, most of the time, quite content with "more-or-less knowing." One can more-or-less know without in any way being immune to error. Perhaps there is wisdom in settling for the more modest achievement of more-or-less knowing.

Words

ONE DAY I ARRIVED at St. Mary's with a copy of *Gulliver's Travels* under my arm and a pack on my back. I started reading to my class the following passage:

We next went to the school of languages, where three professors sat in consultation upon improving that of their own country.

The first project was to shorten discourse, by cutting polysyllables into one, and leaving out verbs and participles, because, in reality, all things imaginable are but nouns.

The other project was a scheme for entirely abolishing all words whatsoever, and this was urged as a great advantage in point of health, as well as brevity. For it is plain, that every word we speak is, in some degree, a diminution of our lungs by corrosion, and, consequently, contributes to the shortening of our lives. An expedient was therefore offered, "that, since words are only names for things, it would be more convenient for all men to carry about them such things as were necessary to express a particular business they are to discourse on" . . . which has only this inconvenience attending it, that, if a man's business be very great, and of various kinds, he must be obliged, in proportion, to carry a greater bundle of things upon his back, unless he can afford one or two strong servants to attend him. I have often beheld two of those sages almost sinking under the weight of their packs, like pedlars among us; who, when they met in the street, would lay down their loads, open their sacks, and hold conversation for an hour together, then put up their implements, help each other to resume their burdens, and take their leave . . .

Another great advantage proposed by this invention was that it would serve as a universal language, to be understood in all civilised nations, whose goods and utensils are generally of the same kind, or nearly resembling . . . [1]

Part way into the passage I realized that the vocabulary was somewhat beyond my hearers and the style rather alien to them, so I paraphrased it. Once the kids had the idea from this passage of "talking with things," I took about twenty assorted objects from my own backpack, including these items, which I passed around the class for inspection:

toy police car	ballpoint pen
"Danger Mouse" figure	piece of paper

1. Jonathan Swift, *Gulliver's Travels*, pt. III, chap. V, in *The Works of Jonathan Swift*, 2nd ed. (London: Bickers, 1883), pp. 223–225.

toy biplane	enormous house-key
toy revolver	several toy soldiers
toy chick	wristwatch
rubber band	several coins

Then I told the children about a game we were going to play. Volunteers from among them (as things turned out, all but two volunteered) were each to think up a sentence they would be able to "say," using objects from my pack. They were to write the sentence down on a piece of paper, fold the paper over, and pass it to me. Then one at a time they were to "say" their sentence to the class, and the class would try to guess what the sentence was. I would write the guesses on the board, and we would then compare them with the written sentence.

Immediately Martin registered the objection that there would be no object to show for *and*. I told him that was an excellent point, and we would return to it in the discussion to follow, but that first we were going to play the game.

The children played it with high spirits. They chose for themselves rather long, episodic sentences. (If I were playing, I would pick much simpler ones.) Many had to do with a revolver—somebody shoots somebody or threatens to do so. Clearly the toy revolver was the most popular object in the collection from my pack. (I have played this game with adult classes; the revolver tends to be popular with them, too.)

The children were amazingly successful at conveying their sentences to the class. No doubt one reason for their success was that they made skillful use of pantomime, something that was not really supposed to be part of the game. This game was so popular that most of our class time was taken up getting through the volunteered sentences. When we finally began the discussion, most of the children had to leave to catch the early bus or for other obligations.

We began the discussion with Martin's point about there being no object named by *and* and hence nothing to show or point to to say "and." David-Paul reminded us that he had used *and* in his sentence (actually several children had used sentences with *and*); he said he had "sort of acted it out so that people could find out that that meant *and*."

"So it wouldn't just be objects that we were using," I said.

"No," he agreed, "you'd have to do some acting."

By this time everyone except Donald, David-Paul, and me had left. The three of us carried on for a while by ourselves. Donald suggested a way of communicating that wouldn't involve speaking. Instead, it would consist in picking out words and pointing to them—for example, to *and* in the blurb on the paperback book I had brought along in my pack. I agreed that that would be a way of using language without speaking.

"Then they'll be saying that you shouldn't read because it corrodes the brain," said David-Paul, mischievously recalling the rationale given in *Gulliver* for using objects instead of words.

Me: "But what about the idea of using objects instead of words?"

David-Paul: "If you said . . ."—he picked up several objects, one at a time—"nobody would understand what that meant."

Me: "So you'd need to do some acting as well?"

David-Paul: "I don't think just with the objects you could do it."

Donald: "And you'd need an awful lot of objects. You'd need thousands of things."

After a little more discussion along these lines, David-Paul introduced an example. An imaginative use of examples is one of the most important techniques for making progress in an abstract discussion like this one. I often encourage adults to cultivate the habit of thinking of examples. To David-Paul this habit seemed inborn.

"Suppose you wanted to say," he suggested, " 'Go to the refrigerator to get some butter.' You'd have to walk and get the refrigerator and pick it up!"

I suggested the expedient of using a toy refrigerator, but I did not, at this stage, allude to the ambiguity that using toys might introduce—that is, the ambiguity between referring to a real refrigerator, of which the toy is only a model, and referring to a toy refrigerator, of which the particular toy would be a sample. Instead I concentrated on the problem of expressing imperatives.

"How could you say, '*Go* to the refrigerator,' " I asked, "without acting?"

David-Paul: "You couldn't. But you could go to the refrigerator and open it up and point to the butter. And they might understand."

Me: "Why wouldn't they think the sentence is 'There's butter in the refrigerator'?"

"Yeah," said David-Paul and fell silent, but only temporarily.

"Maybe it would be different," he said a moment

later, "if we were taught as babies what all this meant."

Donald: "Yeah, if it was natural not to talk and natural to act out with objects, no . . . not act . . . you don't know how to act, but *show* the objects. It would be an awful lot of trouble. But it probably would be possible to do it."

Me: "What would be the difference between stating something and asking a question?"

Donald: "It would be hard."

David-Paul: "It would be very hard."

Donald: "You could, of course, pick up a question mark and say, '*Uh!*'" Donald's idea was that we could have a cardboard or plastic cutout of a question mark; it could be picked up and used whenever a sentence was supposed to be a question.

David-Paul's face suddenly lit up. "What would happen," he asked excitedly, "when you want to say, 'What is the subject [under discussion]?' You couldn't, because, I mean, there is nothing there which is substantial, really . . ."

David-Paul's point was extremely good. To ask what the subject under discussion is, is not to ask of anything in particular whether it is being discussed. So the idea of pointing or showing can't get a toehold. No doubt it is a mistake to suppose that 'subject of discussion' in the sentence 'What is the subject of discussion?' *names* anything at all. In any case it does not name anything that can be pointed to or shown.

David-Paul seemed to speak for both himself and Donald when he sighed and said, in summary, "It would be a very primitive way of living [to speak this way]. You couldn't ask all these questions. I think the way we're living now is the best way. It would be very hard to change that."

The next week I brought along a story that paraphrased the *Gulliver* passage and incorporated most of the previous week's discussion. To encourage further thought on this topic I added the following conclusion:

> "You know, I think the Gulliver story is meant to be a joke," suggested Fiona. "The writer of the story was probably making fun of the idea that words take the place of the things they name. I think he wanted us to see that words are not just substitutes for things."
>
> "Hey, maybe that's right," said Freddie with a smile. "I hadn't thought of it that way."
>
> Freddie's face went solemn again. "Fiona," he said, "what *are* words, anyway?"

At Freddie's final question there was a loud guffaw from Daniel, who then repeated, derisively, the question, "What are words?"

Esther: "What's so funny about that, Daniel?"

Daniel: "Fancy someone saying, 'What's a word?' "

Richard, who had joined the class in January, when he was about to turn nine years old, added his voice. "Come on then, Daniel," he said, "tell us: what's a word?"

Several others then offered Daniel the same challenge. "If you're so smart, tell us, Daniel."

"Well," said Daniel, after a pause, "it's hard to say."

Chorus: "See!"

Under continued pressure Daniel made an effort to

say what a word is. "It's an adjective, or something," he began.

"That's part of a word," said David-Paul. "That's not what a word *is*." I assume he meant that an adjective is one *kind* of word.

There was more conversational byplay and then, trying to encourage Daniel as much as I could, I asked him whether he thought he could explain to somebody, in a way that would be helpful, what a word is.

Daniel: "Well, kind of . . . No. I don't know."

I was tempted to launch into a little homily at this point on how our impasse was typical of philosophical discussions. One begins with what looks like a very simple question, 'What's a word?' 'What is time?' 'What is it to know something?' The question is so basic that answering it, one supposes, will be easy. But after a little reflection, one comes to realize that answering the question in a helpful way will not be easy; it may not even be possible. Does one then not know what words are, or what time is, or what it is to know something?[2]

I was tempted to say all this, but I resisted the temptation. I contented myself with saying to Daniel, "It's pretty hard, isn't it?"

Richard agreed. "Yeah, it's quite hard. You can't describe a word."

Daniel was glad for a way out. "That's what I mean," he said. "You can't describe a word."

Richard wanted to know whether the story was finished. I said I didn't know, what did he think?

2. See Ludwig Wittgenstein, *The Blue and Brown Books* (Oxford: Blackwell, 1969), pp. 26–27.

Richard: "Because we could have another bit about what words are."

"We could," I agreed; "how would it go?"

Esther pointed out that it was already twenty minutes past three, ten minutes until the end of the period.

"Do you mean," I asked, "that we can't settle what words are in ten minutes?"

"No, we can't," she said firmly.

I cajoled the kids a bit, and the discussion heated up immediately.

Martin: "Words are just natural. You can't help them."

David-Paul: "Words aren't natural."

Martin: "How could we have this conversation now if we didn't have words?"

Me: "We couldn't."

David-Paul: "Words aren't natural. If your mother didn't say anything to you, you would just go on going, 'Waa, waa, waa, gaa, gaa, gaa . . .' "

Martin: "It was natural for your mother to speak, wasn't it?"

Martin's reply was perfect, given the point about naturalness he was insisting on. But David-Paul was undaunted. "That's because," he said, "her mother taught her to speak and her mother taught her to speak. And that goes back to when the first words came, like 'Umm, umm, wuh, wuh, . . .' "

Immediately the others began making primitive sounds. Over the din I pressed a question aimed at keeping the discussion going. "So how," I asked, "do you think people got started using words?"

David-Paul: "They needed to have something to show instead of just pointing." Was this a return to the suggestion in *Gulliver* that words are just substitutes for the things they name? Perhaps.

The idea of how language might have got started suddenly gripped Richard's imagination. "Yeah, how did people make up words?" he mused. "People can't just invent words. They couldn't say, 'We just made this marvelous invention—*words*.' "

I wanted to ask him why not. Was it because they wouldn't have the words to do that? Or was it because words are not the right sort of thing to invent? Or was it because one couldn't have the idea of *inventing* words unless one already had the idea of words, and then there would be nothing to invent?

Though I very much wanted to explore Richard's point, there was so much confusion at this point, so many people talking at once, that I had all I could do to bring about some order again. The noise and confusion also made it impossible for me to transcribe anything from that part of the tape.

When the class finally settled down a bit, Richard was saying, "Words started in grunts and then . . . I don't know, then suddenly . . ."

I think Richard was onto the idea that you couldn't conceive of what a word is if there weren't already words. So you couldn't invent them; they would just have to happen naturally.

Something like that was Martin's idea. "You're born with words," he said, adopting an almost moralistic tone, "and you're obviously expected to use them."

There followed an animated discussion on whether dogs or other animals use words. The connection with what had gone before seemed to be that if words were natural for human beings, one could expect them to be natural for other creatures as well.

Martin: "They have their own words."

David-Paul: "How do you know?"

Ise: "Well, why do dogs bark? Do they do it for the *fun* of it?"

David-Paul: "But they aren't saying things like *the*, *a*, . . ."

Ise (and several others): "They are."

David-Paul: "All the barks are the same. They're not what you would call words, Ise."

Martin: "Dogs probably think that what we use are not words, in their sense of 'words'."

I thought here of Wittgenstein's saying, "If a lion could talk, we could not understand him."[3] Wittgenstein presumably meant that our language is essentially so set in our way of life that we can recognize things as words of a language only if we share to a significant degree the form of life of the creature that produces those things. If the forms of life are radically different, there is no basis for understanding the creature's words. It is significant that Wittgenstein chose a lion for his point, not a dog. We have, of course, integrated dogs into *our* way of life in many significant respects. We have, we think, a much better understanding of what life is like for a dog than for, say, a lion, or a bat![4]

Speaking of the bark of a dog, David-Paul said, "It

3. Ludwig Wittgenstein, *Philosophical Investigations* (Oxford: Blackwell, 1967), pt. II, sec. xi, p. 223.

4. See Thomas Nagel, "What Is It Like to Be a Bat?" *Philosophical Review* 83 (1974), 435–450.

could mean a number of different things, like 'I'm hungry,' 'I'm tired,' but they don't have different tones and things like that."

Esther: "I've got three dogs, and they go like *this*"— she imitated a variety of dog sounds, rather convincingly—"and they are words for them. But we can't find out what they are. We can't detect them."

David-Paul had the last comment: "What I'm trying to point out is that they *do* speak. But it's not words."

With that remark it was three-thirty. We certainly hadn't settled what words are in ten minutes. But goaded by an interesting thought experiment from *Gulliver's Travels*, we had canvassed some very interesting thoughts on words and the languages they make up. As a colleague remarked to me later, we had also recapitulated, in telescopic form, much of the history of theories of language.

Time Travel

ONE DAY MARTIN SUGGESTED that it would be nice to have a story with some mystery in it. I said I would try to oblige. It occurred to me that the idea of time travel might be a way of introducing mystery. I was quite confident all the children would have read, heard, or seen on TV some story in which characters travel back in time, and perhaps forward as well; the idea would be quite familiar to them. Yet it is an idea that is philosophically very perplexing.

I suppose most professional philosophers these days assume that the idea of time travel cannot be made logically coherent. If they are right, there is no point in asking whether anybody has ever moved around in time, or how hard it would be to bring off a trip into the past or the future; such a thing would be logically impossible.

A few philosophers have actually bothered to marshal arguments to show that the idea of time travel is logically incoherent. But since that effort merely supports what most philosophers assume to be correct anyway, and no philosophically powerful defender of the coherence of the idea has emerged, the critical and destructive efforts have not excited much attention. It has been left to the writers of fiction to paper over the conceptual and logical difficulties as well as they can.

There is, however, one fly in this otherwise quite numbing ointment. Kurt Gödel, arguably the greatest logician of the twentieth century, and one of the really great logicians of all time, once offered a formula for calculating the fuel that would be required for time travel.[1] Gödel maintained that despite the paradoxes introduced by the idea of time travel (for example, a man might "travel into the near past of those places where he has himself lived . . . find a person who would be himself at some earlier period of his life . . . [and] do something to this person which, by his memory, he knows has not happened to him"),[2] still, we cannot rule out the possibility on logical grounds alone. If the greatest logician of our century thought the idea not ridiculous, then there is reason for the rest of us to take it with some seriousness.

Reflecting on these matters and wanting to meet Martin's request for a story with some mystery in it, I made up one called "The White Door," which began this way:

Freddie and Angus walked down the dark passageway. Clang! The big door through which they

1. Kurt Gödel, "A Remark about the Relationship between Relativity Theory and Idealistic Philosophy," in *Albert Einstein: Philosopher-Scientist*, vol. 2, ed. P. A. Schilpp (New York: Harper and Row, 1959), p. 561 n. 11.
2. Ibid., pp. 560–561.

had just come slammed shut. They heard the turn of a key in the lock.

"Freddie, I think we've been locked in," said Angus nervously.

"There must be a way out at the other end," replied Freddie uncertainly.

The passage was barely lit. As the boys walked along it, becoming more and more frightened, they came alongside a huge, white, iron door with a big brass handle and a very large combination lock. On the door, in large red letters, were the words, 'Extremely Dangerous—Keep Out'. In small black letters underneath were the words 'MOD Time Project'.

"What do you suppose is in there?" whispered Freddie.

"I don't know," answered Angus very slowly. "I think 'MOD' stands for 'Ministry of Defense.' But what could be dangerous about a time project?"

"You've got me," said Freddie. "Let's get out of here."

The boys walked quickly past the white door and made it to the end of the passageway just as a man in a blue uniform appeared, holding a ring of keys. He was obviously locking the building up for the night. "Hallo, what are you boys doing here?" he asked, with annoyance.

"We're supposed to be meeting my sister, Fiona," explained Angus; "she works in the Science Library."

"You're in the wrong building, then," said the man. "You want the building next door. This is the Laboratory of Applied Physics."

"Oh, thanks," said Angus, greatly relieved to be getting out of that spooky place.

As the boys slipped past the guard, Freddie stopped, screwed up his courage, and blurted out, "S-sir, wh-what's in the room behind the white door marked 'Extremely Dangerous'?"

"Oh, that," laughed the guard in a slightly sinister voice; "You wouldn't want to be going in there; your parents wouldn't see anything of you again."

Freddie persisted. "Why not?" he asked.

The guard got serious. He bent over and lowered his voice. "That, my boys," he explained carefully, "is an experimental time machine; if you got shut up in there and set the dials right, you wouldn't be living in 1982 anymore, it might be 1882, or 1915, or . . . who knows when."

"Gosh," said Freddie, "really?"

"You'd better be getting over to the Science Library," said the guard. "You wouldn't want to be messing around with any time machine, now would you?"

"Thanks," said Freddie; he and Angus headed for the building next door.

When Freddie and Angus encounter Alice and Fiona in the Science Library, they report their find with great excitement. Alice, in a pattern by now quite firmly established and recognized by the children in my class, pooh-poohs the idea of time travel.

"A time machine!" she laughed. "Great! and you believed the guard!" Freddie began to lose his temper. "Oh, you're such a know-it-all," he said angrily. "I'd laugh if you got caught in that machine and ended up in . . . 1782."

"It's impossible," said Alice calmly. "If you think about it you can figure it out for yourself. It couldn't happen. If I went back to 1782 there would be someone who was eighteen years old in 1782, who would then have been born in . . . 1764, but who, being me, would have been born in 1964. It's impossible for one and the same person to have been born in 1964 and also to have been born two hundred years earlier. Whatever there is behind that white door, it isn't a time machine. You can know that without even looking. You can know it just by thinking. The guard was having fun with you."

Freddie was boiling with anger. His older sister was very hard to take. She was so conceited! But as he cooled off, he began to think about what she had said. Was she right? Could we really know, without even looking, that there was no time machine behind the white door? That whatever 'MOD Time Project' meant, it didn't mark a place where you could travel through time? We could know that if we could know that time travel is impossible. But can we be sure of that? Is there a way that it could be possible that even smart Alice hadn't thought of?

As it turned out, the day I brought this story-beginning into class coincided with a visit to the city by the Duke of Edinburgh. Martin and several other members of my class, being "first-line" choristers in the cathedral choir, were dispatched to a local hotel to sing for the duke and his entourage. Our class, with reduced numbers and some feeling of having been left behind, was much less fruitful in producing a good discussion than I had hoped it would be.

Still, we soldiered on. Esther took the lead.

Me: "What about Alice's reasoning?"

Esther: "She doesn't know . . . They should take Alice and Fiona and shove them through the white door . . ."

Esther clearly had developed an antipathy to Alice. "She always thinks she's right," Esther said, "and half the time she's wrong."

But what about *this* time? Esther thought Alice was wrong this time, too. It soon became clear that Esther was a fan of time-travel literature, so she was motivated to think Alice wrong. Esther's way of dealing with Alice's argument was to shove Alice in the time machine and show her that her conclusion was wrong.

I pressed Esther and the others on the details of Alice's reasoning. I pointed out that it seemed to turn on whether one person could be born twice. ("If time travel were possible, one person would be born twice; one person couldn't be born twice; therefore, time travel isn't possible.") I then asked the kids whether one person could be born twice. Neil, Daniel, and Ise said, "No." Esther said, "Yes."

Esther: "We might have been born before. We don't know. We might have been born in Victorian days . . . We say Jesus is coming again. So Jesus might be born twice. Who can tell?"

Later in the discussion I got a nice response from Daniel when I asked the kids to suppose we had a machine that could take us back to 1940.

Daniel: "Yeah, take you back to 1940. How many miles away is 1940?"

Daniel's question might be offered as a way of ridiculing, or rejecting, the idea of time travel. But the ruminations of Gödel I mentioned earlier, which are based on Einstein's theory of relativity, suggest that in some conceivable worlds there could be a literal answer to Daniel's question. (". . . by making a round trip on a rocket ship in a sufficiently wide curve, it is possible in these worlds to travel into any region of the past, present, and future, and back again, exactly as it is possible in other worlds to travel to distant parts of space.")[3] I considered, but rejected, the idea of introducing relativity theory into our discussion.

The main point that emerged from the discussion that day was Esther's suggestion that Alice's argument failed because rebirth is not impossible. Here is the way I incorporated that point in the continuation of the story:

> Going home together in the dark, Freddie and Angus talked about Alice and what she had said.
>
> "She doesn't know," said Angus; "if only we could take Alice and Fiona and shove them through that big, white door!"
>
> Freddie was more hesitant. "Maybe she does know," he conceded. "Maybe she knows time travel is impossible. If she knows that, then she knows that whatever is on the other side of that white door, it isn't a functioning time machine, and if she was shoved into the room, whatever happened, it wouldn't really be going back in time."
>
> "But is her reasoning any good?" persisted Angus. "What's this about one person being born in 1964 and also two hundred years earlier?"

3. Ibid., p. 560.

"Yeah, that was her example, all right," agreed Freddie. "But wait! Do we know that's impossible? What about—what's it called?—reincarceration?"

"Reincarnation," suggested Angus.

"Yes, that's it!" Freddie went on, excitedly. "You hear stories about people living a second life. I saw something about that on TV one time."

"So did I," said Angus. "Remember, we talked about it. It was someone who said he had lived before, a very long time ago. And then he was killed in a battle."

"Some people think there isn't any such thing," admitted Freddie. "They think the stories are just made up. But it's not impossible, is it? And if it's not impossible, then what Alice said, that one person couldn't be born in 1964 and also two hundred years ago, is wrong. We don't know that it happens. But if it's not impossible, then time travel is not impossible. Oh boy! I can't wait till I tell her that."

"I hope you win the argument," said Angus supportively, "but probably Alice will just think of some other reason to say that time travel is impossible. Arguing with Alice *and winning* is what's really impossible. What I'd like to do is go behind that door."

"Yeah," agreed Freddie, "that would be fun. But suppose we *really* went back in time." Freddie shivered at the thought. "That would be scary!" he said in a half-whisper.

The Christmas holiday followed that session, and it was some time before we got back again to time travel and "The White Door." Though I had the continuation of the story ready to use in January, I decided to start with "Cheese and Grass" instead. In March, though, we returned to time travel. The story was new to the choristers who had been absent from class the first time, including Martin, whose request for a story with some mystery in it had inspired the story in the first place, and to Richard, who had joined us in January.

The response to my continuation was extremely lively. Unfortunately, the batteries in my tape recorder ran down during the class. I discovered with intense disappointment when I got home that I had no record of the extremely rich discussion that had ensued. I did try to write down the gist of the discussion as best I could; but from past experience I was entirely confident that my memory was but a pale and sketchy replica of the original.

Early on in the discussion David-Paul expressed great skepticism about the possibility of time travel. Donald took up Esther's defense of the idea. Before the telephone was invented, Donald said, one would have thought it impossible to talk to someone thousands of miles away. He suggested that we have no more reason to think time travel impossible than we would have had to think long-distance conversations impossible.

The analogy was apt. Before the invention of the radio and the telephone, talking to someone who is hundreds of miles out of earshot may have seemed not just a physical impossibility, but a logical impossibility as well. After all, one might say that it is logically impossible to hear someone who is out of earshot, that is, out of hearing range. Now, of course, we might say that 'out of hearing range' has two meanings—'out of natural, or unaided, hearing range' and 'out of the range of even aided hearing.' I'm not at all sure that it is good to try to distinguish meanings in this way; but, in any case, this is not a distinction anyone would have thought to make before the invention of the radio and the telephone. Might there be similar moves that would render the apparent contradictions of time travel equally innocuous?

Donald himself did not spell out the aptness of his analogy. Nevertheless, he did choose a very good analogy. He also made another point. Skepticism about time travel takes the form of asking, smugly, "How could it be done?" But one could have asked that about long-distance conversations, too; moreover, even today, most of us are unable to explain how long-distance conversations are possible. Radio and television transmissions seem especially magical, even to those of us who have grown up with them.

At some point in the discussion Martin picked up the skeptical side. He announced that for time travel to be possible, the whole world would have to go back in time. (Richard suggested he had been watching the film *Superman*, in which the hero does go back in time by reversing the world's time, indeed, by "running the world back" to an earlier time and then letting it move forward again.)

Martin had an argument in mind. Suppose there were a time machine outside the school, he suggested. Suppose that machine could take someone, say, Freddie, back to 1615. (Martin chose that date because the oldest part of the school was built in 1615, as a bit of stonework over a door indicated.) Suppose, Martin continued, that Freddie was going back to see the school building being built. Then where would he be, Martin asked, while he was doing this?

Martin was trying to get at what he thought was an incoherence in the idea of a certain person, or certain people, but not the whole world, going back in time.

I'm not completely confident that we got clear in the class discussion about what the incoherence was supposed to be. As I tried to spell it out later on, without benefit of a tape recording, I came up with this:

(1) If Freddie could go back independently in time, there would be some time when he was doing this.

(2) If there were some time when Freddie was going back in time, there would be a good answer to the question, asked while he was doing it, 'Where is he now?'

(3) There would be no good answer to the question, asked while he was doing it, 'Where is he now?'

Therefore,

(4) Freddie could not go back independently in time.

Since the argument works equally well for anyone we choose, we may generalize,

(5) No one person could go back independently in time.

Quite obviously, (3) needs support. Martin's idea seemed to be that 'He's in that time machine over there' wouldn't be any good as an answer to the question, 'Where is he now?' for it would commit us to his being in 1983. 'He's in 1615' wouldn't be any good either, Martin reasoned, since, if he were ever *there*, it would have been in 1615, not "now," in 1983. Finally, 'He's nowhere,' Martin reasoned, would be no good, since if he were nowhere he wouldn't be traveling back in time either.

I found this a fascinating argument. Perhaps there is

something like it in the enormous literature on the philosophy of time, but I do not know of anything. To me
it was a novel argument, a jewel to admire and delight
in before going on to assess its worth in the exchange of
ideas.

The next week I came back with this installment,
which was meant to capture Martin's argument:

> Fiona and Alice walked along the road toward the
> science building. Alice's mother had sent them on
> an urgent mission, to find Freddie and Angus.
> Freddie had left a note in his room that said:

>> Dear Family,
>>   Angus and I have gone to the science
>> building to try to get inside the time machine
>> there. If we succeed in traveling back in time,
>> we may not be home for tea. But please don't
>> worry. We promise to return.
>>
>>   Love,
>>   Freddie

> When Freddie's mother read the note, she almost
> passed out. After she got control of herself again,
> she sent Alice and Fiona to look for the boys, then
> called the police.

> As the girls hurried on their way, Alice kept pro-
> ducing arguments to prove that wherever Freddie
> and Angus were, they were not speeding back in
> time. Fiona was not convinced. "You don't really
> know," she said to Alice.

> "It's simply impossible," said Alice.

> "Look," said Fiona, "if somebody had told you
> long before telephones were invented that one day

you could talk to someone thousands of miles away, you would have said that was impossible. Now it happens all the time. Sure, we don't know how anybody could manage to go back in time, but that doesn't mean it is impossible. It may be no more impossible than long-distance telephoning."

"The only way there could be time travel," said Alice firmly, "would be for the whole world to travel in time."

"You must have seen *Superman*," said Fiona.

"I'm serious," said Alice. "Look, imagine there really was a time machine behind that big, white door in the science building. And suppose Freddie and Angus had managed to get in it. Suppose they set the dials to go back two hundred years, to 1783, and then the thing made all kinds of sputtering and whirring noises, and the control panel announced they were in 1783. I ask you, where would they be *now?*"

"In 1783," said Fiona, "where else?"

"No, they couldn't be there *now*," insisted Alice; "if they were *ever* in 1783, they would have been there two hundred years ago, in 1783, not *now*, in 1983."

Fiona was puzzled. "Maybe they'd be nowhere," she suggested.

"If they were nowhere, then they wouldn't be time-traveling either," replied Alive.

"Oh, I suppose they'd be behind that white door in the science building," said Fiona in a third effort to answer Alice's question.

"Then they would still be in 1983," said Alice triumphantly; "you see, there just isn't a good answer to where they'd be. So the whole thing is impossible—unless, of course, the whole world were to go back in time. But then our mums wouldn't need to worry about them; we would all be wherever they are in time."

I asked my kids whether this continuation of the story captured the main argument from last time. There was general agreement that it did. We talked a bit about how the story ought to end.

"What if they opened the white door and found a clock," suggested Martin.

"An electronic clock," said Richard.

"After all," Martin went on, "it just said, 'MOD Time Project.' "

Me: "Is that the way it should end?"

Martin: "I don't know."

Neil: "And then it was all a dream."

Ise: "No, because they could still have this argument in a dream."

I seem not to have responded directly to Ise's comment, but it pleased me very much. If a line of argument is interesting, worth reflecting on, and trying to assess, it doesn't matter whether it appeared in a dream or a story or a book of philosophy.

The class discussion then turned to the problem of determining whether it could be coherent, from the point of view of the time visited, to suppose there were visitors from a later time. The children seemed to think that part could be managed.

David Paul: "We might hear a story from that time about some flying machine which landed and these strange people came out. People might have told their children and they told *their* children—'At one time, in 1783, a space ship landed in so-and-so . . . ' But that wouldn't be now. That would have happened then."

Donald then told a time-travel story.

David-Paul: "If it was going back in time, you'd have to be part of history. If you weren't, you'd be standing there and nobody could see you. You'd be invisible."

So there seemed to be two ways the visit might be shown to be coherent from the point of view of the earlier time. One way would be for it to be clear the mysterious things had already happened long ago that can now be understood as visits by people today to that past time. The other would be for it to be shown that the visitors are invisible to people in the earlier time and play no role in the happenings of the time they visit.

I ended the story this way:

Just at that moment Alice took in the fact that the two small figures in the distance were Freddie and Angus.

"Look who's walking toward us!" shouted Alice. "It's Freddie and Angus!"

Alice didn't know whether to express great happiness and relief that they were all right or to be very stern and tell them how much anxiety they had caused or to pretend that nobody was concerned about them.

"How should we react?" Alice whispered to Fiona without giving any indication to the boys, who were still a long way off, that she had recognized them. "Should we let on that we are relieved, or be cross, or what?"

"Let's let them know how glad we are to see

them," said Fiona, who began immediately to wave to the boys.

"But why should I be relieved?" said Alice. "I had a very good argument to prove that time travel is impossible, so there was nothing to worry about."

"I agree you had an interesting argument," said Fiona, "but I'm not sure I trust my brother's safety to your reasoning ability. I'm jolly glad to see with my own eyes that he's safely here in 1983."

By this time the boys were within hailing distance. But they were obviously not in a happy mood.

"What happened?" asked Fiona excitedly.

"Nothing," said Angus sadly. The boys didn't say much until the little group got near their two homes. Then, reluctantly, Freddie explained.

"That MOD Time Project isn't a time machine at all," he said slowly. "It's an experiment with an electronic clock. The guard who told us there was a time machine behind the white door was a liar and a bum."

"Well, I'm not glad the guard is a bum," said Fiona cheerfully, "but I'm very pleased you're safely here with us in 1983."

"Fiona," protested Alice, "they couldn't be anywhere else; if time travel were possible . . ."

"Aw, shut up!" said Fiona in an unusual burst of temper.

Ethics

Ian (six years) found to his chagrin that the three children of his parents' friends monopolized the television; they kept him from watching his favorite program. "Mother," he asked in frustration, "why is it better for three people to be selfish than for one?"

I decided to make this anecdote, which is taken from my book *Philosophy and the Young Child* (p. 28), the basis for a story-beginning that might encourage a discussion of ethics. Although I knew very little about British television, I had the impression that the children's afternoon show, *The Moomins*, was a bit too juvenile for the members of my class. So I began the story this way:

Freddie settled down into his favorite armchair with a glass of Five Alive and a handful of coconut biscuits. He was ready to watch the latest episode of *The Abbott and Costello Show* on TV. His state of happy relaxation was interrupted by the sound of a car pulling up to the house. Then came the noise of car doors opening and shutting and of voices approaching the front door. Freddie's determined efforts to concentrate on the TV screen were finally frustrated by the sound of the doorbell, followed by the advance of a horde of chattering people.

"Freddie," his mother was saying above the din, "these are the Aitkens—do you remember them?—they're from Plockton. They've had a long journey. Let the little ones have a go at the TV while I put the kettle on for tea. Let's see, this is Sarah, Douglas, and, oh yes, Tom. You children have grown so much I hardly recognize you."

"I want to watch the Moomins," shouted Douglas.

"Yeah," agreed the other two, "let's watch the Moomins."

"Are you sure you wouldn't like to watch Abbott and Costello?" asked Freddie as politely as he could.

"No-o-o," they replied in a chorus. "Let's watch the Moomins."

Douglas, who acted as the leader of the group, walked calmly to the TV, reached for the knob, and switched the program to the Moomins.

Freddie got up sadly and went out to the kitchen.

"Why the sad face?" said Freddie's mother, as she filled the kettle. "I know they're younger than you, but they're nice kids, really. And their mum and dad are very old friends of your mum and dad. Please be nice to them."

"But they want to watch the Moomins!" said Freddie in disbelief.

"I'm sorry," said Freddie's mother; "I know you

can't stand that program. But think of it this way. Three people are being made happy instead of just one."

Freddie reflected a moment. "Mother," he said, slowly and deliberately, "why is it better for three people to be selfish than for one?"

In the original anecdote the rejection of utilitarianism (the view that one should always do what will maximize happiness) is only implicit. In the story-beginning above, Freddie's mother presents this quite directly, though of course she doesn't say she is stating an ethical principle; she just invites Freddie to note that as things have worked out, "three people are being made happy instead of just one."

One nice thing about this sort of example is that it both encourages generalization and invites attention to a specific kind of case. Thus the ratio, three to one, encourages one to quantify benefits and losses and bring these under some general principle. On the other hand, it is so easy to feel outraged at the thought of being invaded by a horde of boors and made to surrender one's most basic privileges that one's intuitions of fair and foul play are immediately awakened and set against the cool calculation of impersonal benefits and losses. The mores of hospitality are also called into play, although these do not have an unambiguously moral significance.

David-Paul immediately reacted to the host-guest aspect of the case. "They're going to visit your house once," he said. "You have to make a nice impression." It wasn't clear whether he thought making a nice impression was a moral requirement or simply in the host's self-interest.

Martin was outraged. "It's not very nice to come into someone's house," he pointed out, "and say"—here he broke into a chant—'We-want-to-watch-the-Moomins.' "

David-Paul was ready with the first of many considerations he mentioned in an effort to get clear about what would be fair. "By the way," he said, "isn't it a bit mean, though, because there are three people; with three people, they could all play together."

It was a very practical consideration. Three people who already know each other can entertain each other quite easily. A lone person, who doesn't yet know the others, may have a larger claim on scarce entertainment resources.

Martin continued to express outrage. "I would hate it," he said, "if I was watching TV happily and suddenly somebody comes up the driveway with three weird children. The mum says, 'Go and watch TV,' and they come up and say, 'We want to watch the Moomins.' I mean, they could easily have watched what Freddie was watching."

David-Paul: "They have to respect other people's rights as well. The Moomins are on almost every day."

Here was another relevant consideration. One has less claim, David-Paul seemed to assume, to pursue an activity that could as well be pursued on any number of other occasions than to do something for which there are fewer opportunities.

Richard: "Are the Moomins a serial?"

Me: "Yes."

Richard: " 'Cause *The Abbott and Costello Show* is a serial as well. So it doesn't matter. They can watch them some other time."

Richard was suggesting that David-Paul's point doesn't really help us come to a conclusion in this case. Since both programs are serials, each could be watched on many other occasions.

Everyday ethics, like the common law, arbitrates disputes and conflicts of interest by appeal to cases, as interpreted, perhaps, by low-level "maxims," or "rules of law." This arbitration may succeed without anyone's having to show that the reasoning fits into some coherent system that will resolve all conceivable disputes. Of course someone might insist that disputes resolved in this fashion are not resolved correctly unless the resolution can be shown to fall appropriately under some absolutely general principle or to fit properly into some universal system.

I was interested that none of my kids seemed attracted by the pull to general theory. They had very strong feelings about the case I had presented, and they were quick to recall relevant experiences from their own lives, to make up analogous cases, and to extract low-level maxims from these real and imagined examples. But they found utilitarianism unattractive, and they were not inclined to search for any similarly high-level principle or theory to replace utilitarianism.

"What about this argument," I asked again, trying to get them to take utilitarianism seriously, "that, if we let the three visitors have their way, three people will be made happy instead of just one?"

Martin: "It's not really fair if three people get what they want and leave one person out. That one person will feel very hurt."

So utilitarianism (unless, perhaps, applied in a much more imaginative and sophisticated way than I had suggested) conflicts with fairness. But how does one get clear about what fairness requires?

David-Paul, as usual, was ready with another relevant consideration. "It depends on the ages," he said. "If one person is really old and the others are small, then the younger children should be allowed to watch their program."

Richard: "No. You should respect your elders."

Me: "You have two opposite principles."

Richard: "Suppose there was someone my age . . ."

David-Paul: "And someone fifteen comes along and wants to watch a mathematical program. Of course you don't want to watch that. He should let you watch your program, unless he was doing a special project."

Me: "Richard, do you think the younger kids should *always* defer to the older kids?"

Richard: "Unless it's something dangerous."

David-Paul: "It depends on the frequency of the program, really. And how old you are. If there is only one program a week and you're big, then you can watch that. If you're small, the same thing. But then if you both have serials, it should be the younger person that gets to watch more. Unless there is something coming on a sequel, and then you ask the other person whether he could watch his at another time."

A little later David-Paul brought out other considerations: "It makes a difference whether you have a sister or a brother, or if you have visitors. A sister or brother could watch the program anytime, really. Because they [the programs] often come twice. But if it's someone who just comes to your house, you should let them choose. And if it's somebody who doesn't have a television, they should be able to choose."

Even when there was general agreement on a maxim, the children seemed not to want to stop there; they wanted to awaken the moral sentiment that gives force to the maxim. Thus there was general agreement when David-Paul said, "I think you should be nice to people who are visiting."

But Martin thought it important to add, "You might have some visitors you've never seen before. And they say, 'Are you watching this?' And you say, 'Yes.' And they go away and never come back again."

I kept introducing utilitarianism; the kids kept rejecting it.

David-Paul: "But if there was this really disgusting program in which people are taking out people's hearts and transplanting them and things like that, and just this one person didn't want to watch it, he would have to move out of the room. That would be like saying, 'I don't want you in this room.' "

Donald, and later Esther, added a note of stoic resignation to the discussion. "If I'd been in Freddie's shoes," Donald said at one point, "I wouldn't exactly have minded it." Later on he added, "I would say, 'They only want to watch this one and then tomorrow they'll be gone and I can watch my program next time.' "

David-Paul: "But [it says in the story] it was the last program."

We checked and found it said that Freddie was ready to watch "the latest" episode of *The Abbott and Costello Show*.

Me: "Suppose it was the last. What difference would it make?"

Esther: "None, really."

David-Paul: "Just say that somebody was just about

to be blown up by the atomic bomb. You would want to find out if he escaped or not."

Martin: "Yeah, just wait till the end of this program."

I made up a continuation of the story that incorporated some of the many considerations the children had raised in our rich discussion together. This installment was pretty much a failure, though. It didn't spark off any new ideas, nor did it bring the problem to resolution.

After we read the new installment together and tried unsuccessfully to push the discussion further, I set the kids the task of drawing up rules for the use of a TV in a school boarding house. The resulting dialogue replayed much of what had been said the previous week, so I dropped the Moomins for a while. Every week Richard would ask, "Are we going to finish the Moomins today?" "No," I would reply, lamely, "not today, maybe next week."

Finally, some two months later, we did get back to the Moomins. I had decided that since I had been unable to get anyone to defend utilitarianism, it might be interesting to see whether some other, absolutely general ethical principle would be more satisfactory to my kids. Thinking that the Golden Rule would be the principle they would be most likely to accept, I decided to play devil's advocate and see if one or more of my kids would defend that hallowed principle. Here is what I wrote:

"That was a good question you put to Mum yesterday," said Alice to Freddie the next morning over breakfast.

"What question was that?" asked Freddie.

"You said, 'Why is it better for three people to be selfish than for one?' Mum didn't know what to say."

"Thanks," said Freddie. "Weren't those kids awful?"

"Real twerps," agreed Alice, "but it was good you showed up the rule about making as many people happy as possible. That rule isn't right. But then there aren't any good rules to tell you what to do in hard situations."

"What about the Golden Rule?" asked Freddie.

"Oh, you mean—'Do unto others as you would have them do unto you'?" said Alice.

"Yeah," said Freddie.

"Well, just think about it," said Alice; "it means we ought to treat other people as we would like to be treated if we were the other people. Now think of those ridiculous kids who took over the TV and insisted on watching the Moomins."

"Yeah," said Freddie, "they should have thought about whether they would like some strange kids to break into their house, take over their TV, and start watching some program they didn't like. I felt like bopping them in the face."

"Okay," said Alice, "but what about you? According to the Golden Rule you should treat them as you would like to be treated if you were one of them. But if you came into a strange house, and your favorite program were the Moomins, you would want the kid who lived there to let you watch the Moomins, right? So if you treated those twerps the way you would like to be treated if you were one of them, you would turn over the TV to them and let them watch the Moomins, right? But, as you realize, that's a lot of bunk. The Golden Rule is no good."

Freddie didn't know what to say. He had thought the rule about making as many people happy as possible was a bad rule. If you followed that rule you might make lots of kids happy and leave one kid sad all his life. That wouldn't be right. But Freddie had thought the Golden Rule was okay. Maybe Alice was right. Maybe the Golden Rule was no better than the other one. Could it be that the Golden Rule was really no good?

In fact no one in my class at St. Mary's seemed at all bothered by this attack on the Golden Rule. Donald said that personally he had found the Golden Rule disappointing. He had often tried it, he said, and although sometimes it "worked," often it didn't. He seemed to mean that often it didn't lead either to fairness or to any sense of satisfaction.

David-Paul's comment was, "If everybody used it, it would be brilliant." In finishing the story I used his idea.

"The Golden Rule would be a good rule if everybody followed it," said Angus.

"But everybody doesn't," replied Freddie quickly. "In fact, most people don't."

"I know," said Angus. "The most you can say is, do what you can to encourage everybody, including yourself, to follow the Golden Rule."

"That's pretty good," said Freddie, "in fact, that's

a sort of a rule, too. What do you think of that rule, Alice?"

But Alice had left, as Freddie quickly discovered.

"I'll have to ask Alice about your rule," said Freddie. "I don't see how she can say that your rule is no good—but you can never tell about Alice. She finds something wrong with everything."

The Future

ONE DAY ESTHER ASKED for a story about a dog. She said she liked dogs in general, but dachshunds especially. I promised to bring a story-beginning about a dog for the next class. Here is what I produced.

Freddie bent down over the box and carefully pulled back the blanket that was partly covering Angus's new little brown puppy. While Freddie stroked the soft, warm body, Angus smiled with pride. When Angus had first announced he was going to get a dachshund puppy, Freddie hadn't been so sure he would like it. What Freddie wanted was a Labrador. But in fact he did like Angus's dog; he liked it very much.

"I think she's totally worn out," commented Angus. "When we first got her home, she ran all over the house, leaving little puddles everywhere. Finally she had some milk and then she collapsed."

"Is this the first day she's been without her mother and her brothers and sisters?" asked Freddie.

Just then the little dachshund began to bark excitedly in her high-pitched voice. Angus took a turn at stroking her, and gradually she quieted down.

"Yeah, it must be pretty hard on her," said Angus. "I wonder what she's thinking, being in such a strange place. Maybe she thinks she'll go back to her mother tomorrow."

"I don't suppose she can think that," said Freddie.

"Why not?" asked Angus.

"Well," explained Freddie, "I suppose that a dog thinks in pictures, like the pictures cartoonists put in the balloons over animals' heads. You couldn't have a picture that meant *tomorrow*, could you? You'd have to use a regular word. It wouldn't need to be the English word; it could be the French word— what is it? We learned it last week in school."

"*Demain*," replied Angus.

"Yeah, *demain*—or a word in some other language. But it couldn't just be a picture. So dogs can't think about tomorrow."

"That's terrible," said Angus, "imagine not being able to think about tomorrow. You wouldn't realize there's a future."

I put in the French word *demain* because I knew that several of the kids were just beginning to learn French. (And they were being introduced to other languages as well. The choristers in the group regularly had to sing in Latin and occasionally in German. Richard later complained to me about the difficulty of learning to pronounce the German for Bach's *Saint John Passion*, which the cathedral choir sang on Good Friday that year.)

The topic of mental representation came to me naturally. I had taught a course on that topic the previous year at the University of Massachusetts. Questions about whether one can think in pictures and, if so, what limitations a picture "vocabulary" imposes, are debated heatedly these days among philosophers, psychologists, and computer scientists. I find that debate fascinating and important. A story about a dog seemed a good way of introducing it to my kids at St. Mary's.

Martin started off the discussion. "Dogs don't need to use the French word *demain*," he said. "They've got their own way, their own language, their own way of saying *tomorrow*."

"How do we know that?" I asked.

Martin paused. "Well," he said, "how often do you hear a dog say *demain?*"

Everybody laughed.

I decided we needed another example. I asked for suggestions of something one might *remember* having done yesterday and also *think* about doing again *tomorrow*. Being in a music school, these kids naturally thought of practicing. Both Ise and Esther were accomplished violinists, and both won a first prize for their age group in a regional contest later that year. So we made our sample thought one about playing the violin.

Me: "Suppose this is my thought—I'm going to play the violin tomorrow. What is it for me to have that thought?"

Martin: "You say to yourself, 'I'm going to play the violin tomorrow.' You don't say it out loud."

Richard: "You have a picture of yourself playing the violin."

Me: "Good. Those are two ways. Richard and Martin have suggested two ways. Now the problem is, if we had only pictures"—on the board I drew a crude sketch of me playing the violin—"what would be the difference between a picture of me playing the violin yesterday and me playing the violin tomorrow?"

Martin: "Well, you can't exactly predict an actual, proper picture of yourself tomorrow, but you can remember yesterday."

Me: "Suppose we had a fancy machine, and we could put it on my head and you could look down there and see what pictures I was seeing in my mind." I tried to dramatize this procedure by pretending to look into such a "mindscope." "And you looked in and said, 'Oh, he's seeing himself playing a violin.' Now the question is, is he thinking of himself playing the violin *yesterday*, remembering playing the violin, *or* is he thinking of playing the violin *tomorrow*, or sometime in the future? What would be the difference in the *picture?*"

Someone: "The picture would be the same."

Richard: "Unless you had your hair cut."

[Laughter]

I think I probably did need a haircut at the time—several kids commented when I later got it cut.

There was, of course, a serious point behind Richard's slightly mischievous suggestion, a point many of the others caught onto right away. One way of representing time is through changes in the persons, places, and things represented. If we can assume that tomorrow is "after the haircut," then anything that portrays me "after the haircut" will portray me tomorrow. Somewhat more carefully, if I am to get my hair cut tomorrow morning, anything that portrays me with my hair cut will, in a suitable context, portray me tomorrow or sometime thereafter.

My transcript suggests that Donald was silent up to this point. But what he said after this suggests he had been thinking all the time.

Donald: "What evidence is there that [dogs] might think about tomorrow? We can't really tell. There is nothing that says, 'Okay, if you look around for what we've been talking about this afternoon you'll see that it's true that dogs can think about tomorrow.' There isn't really any evidence. From what I've heard, there isn't any evidence for the possibility that dogs can think about tomorrow."

I was very pleased to get Donald's redirection of our thinking. To underline his point I tried making it in my own way. "So what Donald is saying is that it would be nice if we had some evidence that they really do think about tomorrow, and then we could ask, 'How do they do it?' But if we don't have any evidence that they do think about tomorrow, why worry about it?"

My paraphrase seemed to win Donald's approval.

I asked what evidence we have that dogs can think about the past. Several kids replied, in various ways, that the only way dogs could learn to do anything right was if they remembered and thought about the past. The suggestion was both natural and very much in need of further examination. But we were virtually at the end of our period. In fact the period ended with Donald reiterating his point about our not having evidence that dogs can think about the future, and Martin musing, "They might say, 'We're going for our daily walk tomorrow.' " As was often the case, Martin had a twinkle in his eye.

The next week I brought along a second installment.

Just then Fiona, Angus's older sister, came into the room. "How do you like our little puppy?" she asked cheerfully.

"She's really nice," said Freddie. "She makes me wish I had one—she's so soft and warm and . . . and funny."

"Funny? Maybe you wouldn't think she was so funny if you had to clean up after her," said Fiona with some irritation. "The first thing she did after she arrived was to piddle all over the house."

"Freddie says dogs can't think about tomorrow," said Angus, still worried about the problem Freddie had raised. "What do you think, Fiona?"

"You mean she's not lying there thinking of the fun she'll have piddling over the carpet tomorrow," said Fiona with a faint smile.

"This is serious," replied Freddie. "Dogs think in pictures. And you can't have a picture that means *tomorrow*. You'd have to have a regular word."

"Dogs have their own way of thinking," said Fiona. "We don't know how they do it."

"But suppose I'm right," persisted Freddie, "suppose they do think in pictures. And suppose we had a machine—sort of like an X-ray machine—that we could put over the puppy's head to see what was in her mind. Suppose we looked at the display screen, like a miniature TV set, and saw the pictures that went through the puppy's mind. Now suppose . . ."

"Wait a minute!" interrupted Fiona. "This is going too fast. Back up, please. Let's start again. Suppose dogs think in pictures. Then what?"

"Suppose," explained Freddie more slowly, "we could see their thoughts, in a machine we put on their heads, maybe. Now suppose we looked in the machine we had put on your puppy's head and we saw a picture of her piddling on the carpet. What would be the difference, *in the picture*, between her remembering piddling on the carpet *yesterday* and her thinking she'll do it *tomorrow?*"

"I guess the picture would be the same," admitted Fiona, "just as my picture in my mind of me playing the violin would be the same whether I was remembering playing the violin yesterday or thinking I would play it tomorrow."

"Unless you planned to get your hair cut first," put in Angus, mischievously.

"What do you mean?" asked Fiona, puzzled.

"If you planned to get your hair cut first, then you'd picture yourself with short hair playing your violin," explained Angus.

"Oh brother!" laughed Fiona. "But Freddie's point is still right. Short hair doesn't *mean* tomorrow. Just looking at the picture—supposing you put Freddie's mindscope on my head—you couldn't tell whether I was remembering that I played my violin just after the *last time* I had my hair cut or thinking I would play it after the *next time* I get it cut."

"So am I right?" asked Freddie eagerly. "If dogs think in pictures, they can't think about tomorrow?"

"It's an interesting problem," agreed Fiona.

"Don't just say that," objected Angus. "That sounds like a grown-up. Say whether you think he's right."

Fiona reflected a moment. "I guess I'd want evidence they *do* think about tomorrow," Fiona said. "If we had good evidence they think about tomorrow, then we could ask how they do it. Otherwise, why worry about it? Maybe thinking about today is enough for them."

Everybody stared at the sleeping puppy.

"Wait," said Angus excitedly, "I don't know about tomorrow, but there is evidence they can think a little bit into the future. I've seen dogs go to the door and paw and bark to be let out. They must be able to think of themselves going outside after someone has opened the door for them."

"Good point," agreed Fiona. "But tomorrow— why would they ever need to think about tomorrow? Maybe just a little peep into the future is all they need."

After we had read the new installment together, the discussion began.

Me: "I added a bit at the end. Remember Donald said, 'What's the evidence they *do* think about tomorrow?' "

Daniel: "What does that mean?"

Me: "What do they *do* that makes us think they *can* think about tomorrow?"

Daniel: "Because we put that thing [the mindscope] on their head."

Me: "But remember, we were asking what the difference would be, *in the picture*, between seeing what the dog was remembering having done and seeing what it was planning to do in the future."

At this point there was a knock on the door. One of the teachers wanted to conduct some business with several of the children. After the interruption I started up the discussion again.

Me: "So we were asking, 'Is there something they do that makes us think *they* think about tomorrow?' I just added a little bit [to the story] that says maybe there is nothing they do that makes us believe they think about *tomorrow*, but there is at least something dogs do that makes us believe they can think a little bit into the future. For example, they go to the door and paw to be let out."

David-Paul: "But maybe they just want to be let out."

Me: "You mean they could do that without thinking about the future?"

David-Paul: "Without thinking of themselves walking outside."

David-Paul's suggestion astounded me. I had been thinking something quite similar myself. I had wondered whether to suggest it, if the occasion seemed appropriate. Tentatively I had decided that the discussion was already complicated enough without adding this point. Then David-Paul, who had missed the previous week's discussion and had just been introduced to our line of thinking, came up, seemingly effortlessly, with the point I had suppressed in myself.

There followed a nice exchange between Donald and David-Paul. As often happened in these discussions, they developed lines of thought somewhat at variance with each other, but close enough for a real debate.

Donald: "It's obvious that they do, that they have some thought of the future. If you've got a dog that's been taught to do something . . . if it didn't have a look at the future . . . it wouldn't know where to go."

David-Paul: "If it's always taken a certain way and knows that way and gets a certain smell, then when it gets there and gets that smell, it will know what to do."

The debate between these two continued for a while. After they had discussed several hypothetical examples, Donald told us about how his dog behaved when he saw Donald packing his bags. ("If he sees me packing my bags and nobody else, he knows I'm coming back to school, or anyway, going away again.")

Eventually David-Paul came to agree with Donald that we have some evidence that dogs can think about the future, but then he asked, "What proof do we have that they think in pictures?"

Me: "That's just a suggestion."

Donald: "I don't reckon they think in pictures; I reckon they know, just the way we do."

Martin: "What would it be like if they couldn't think?"

Me: "What's an example of something living that can't think?"

Several kids: "Plants."

David-Paul: "But we've already talked about them."

At this point the discussion veered off into the consideration of whether *we* can think about the future, and especially, *know* anything about the future. In finishing the story I expanded a bit on the question of how we can think of, say, tomorrow, and ignored the question of what we can know about the future.

"How is it *we* can think of tomorrow?" asked Angus.

"That's easy," replied Fiona, "we can use the word *tomorrow*."

"But what makes that word *mean* tomorrow when I use it?" asked Angus.

"That's a good question," said Freddie. "When I say *Alice*, that word means my sister because I have a picture of my sister in my mind when I use her name. But, as we all agree, you couldn't have a picture of tomorrow, so what makes the word *tomorrow* mean the right thing, when we use it?"

"You guys ask too many questions," said Fiona. "Anybody for tea?"

"Not just now, thanks, Fiona," said Freddie. He paused. Then his face broke into a broad smile. "Maybe tomorrow," he added, grinning.

Developmental Psychology

STEVE, exactly three years old, watched his father eat a banana.

"You don't like bananas, do you, Steve?" said Steve's father.

"No," replied Steve. "If you were me, you wouldn't like bananas either." Steve paused to reflect. "Then," he added after a minute, "who would be the daddy?"

One remarkable thing about this anecdote is that it reveals a three-year-old using correctly the subjunctive mood of the verb *to be*. I questioned Steve's father about that. "Surely," I insisted, "Steve must have said, 'If you *wuz* me, you wouldn't like bananas either.' Nobody will believe that a three-year-old said, 'If you *were* me . . .' "

Steve's father stood his ground. "Then everybody will be wrong," he said calmly. "Steve's words were 'if you were me.' "

Another remarkable thing about this anecdote is that it reveals a three-year-old taking up, imaginatively, the sensibility of another person. Piaget has taught us to suppose that children of that age, and even those who are much older, are highly egocentric.

A third remarkable thing is that the anecdote reveals a three-year-old using a nice bit of reasoning. If we were to make a bit more explicit the reasoning implicit in Steve's remarks, we might come up with something like this:

(1) Anybody who was me would like what I like and would not like what I don't like.

(2) I don't like bananas.

(3) Anybody who was me wouldn't like bananas.

Thus,

(4) If Daddy were me, he wouldn't like bananas either.

It might be a long time before Steve is able to make his reasoning that explicit, or it might not. I don't know. But implicitly anyway, such was Steve's reasoning.

A fourth remarkable thing about this anecdote is that it shows a three-year-old bringing up an interesting puzzle in the logic of counterfactual conditionals. Until about twenty years ago, the logic of counterfactual conditionals was rather poorly understood. Many people were very skeptical that any good sense could be made of it. Now we have quite a good theory of counterfactual conditionals, based upon what is called in technical philosophy "possible-world semantics."

Among the many puzzles that counterfactual conditionals engender, some of the most difficult arise specifically from what are called "counterfactual identicals." We say things like, "If Edward Heath had been Margaret Thatcher, he would have reached an agreement with Argentina over the Falklands." Suppose we grant, for purposes of discussion, anyway, that Mr. Heath might have been much more conciliatory than Mrs. Thatcher could possibly bring herself to be. Why should we say, "If Mr. Heath had been Mrs. Thatcher, he would have reached an agreement"? If he had been Mrs. Thatcher, surely he would have been as tough as nails!

Steve's worry was not exactly that, however. He wasn't worried about whether (1) if the father were Steve, the father would not like bananas, because Steve doesn't, or (2) if the father were Steve, Steve *would* like bananas, because the father does. He happily says to his father something analogous to what you and I would say in such circumstances: "If you were me, you wouldn't like bananas either." What puzzles Steve is roles and role players. If Steve's father were Steve, who would be "the daddy," that is, who would there be to play the father role?

One reason it is hard to respond well to Steve's question is that it is very hard to be clear about what a counterfactual identical is supposed to mean. The very philosophers who made the recent breakthrough on understanding counterfactual statements in general are deeply divided on how to handle counterfactual identicals.

Of course there are appropriate responses to Steve's puzzlement, even if they don't resolve it completely. For example, one might try out the suggestion, "If I were you, Steve, perhaps *my* daddy would be 'the' daddy." It would be interesting to find out what Steve thought of that suggestion.

No widely accepted theory of developmental psychology makes any real place for philosophical thinking in preadolescents. Perhaps one reason is that *spontaneously* philosophical comments and questions in young children, such as Steve's question above and comments and questions I discuss in *Philosophy and the Young Child,* are singular and nonstandard. They are "oddball" comments and questions. Developmentalists, being primarily concerned with the normal and the standard, are almost bound to ignore such remarks and questions on purely methodological grounds.

But what about the *capacity* to do philosophy, which is so richly displayed in the dialogues I conducted with these children at St. Mary's Music School in Edinburgh? Why is this not given any place in the developmentalist's profile of the preadolescent mind? A fully adequate answer to that question would be very complex, and perhaps also very deep. I shall just mention briefly three points that would need to be included in any really adequate response.

First, developmental psychologists are much more likely to concern themselves with the development of capacities that are widely prized in our society than with the development of a capacity that is generally ignored. The ability to think philosophically and to discuss basic questions openly is widely ignored in our society. Most adults give little or no thought to philosophical questions and have no concern for whether philosophy is practiced well or even practiced at all. It is therefore not surprising that developmental psychologists have little to say about whether—and if so, how—children develop the ability to think philosophically and to pursue philosophical questions intelligently.

Second, it is natural to conceive developmental psychology on a biological model, where a mature specimen is taken as the standard toward which the immature individual develops. The developmentalist may then try to determine what stages an individual goes through in reaching maturity for the skill or capacity in question, or perhaps what influences accelerate or retard the attainment of maturity. If developmental psychology is conceived in this way, research on stages of development, or on factors that lead to acceleration or retardation, cannot get started until there is a fairly good sense of what maturity might amount to for this or that skill or capacity. Perhaps the experts do, in fact, have a fairly good sense of what maturity in doing mathematics or common-sense physics amounts to, or what it is to be a mature speaker or writer of English. But nobody has thought about what a reasonable standard of maturity in philosophical thinking and discussion might be, or even whether there is such a thing. In the absence of some notion of maturity for the capacity to engage in philosophical dialogue, developmental psychology, as standardly conceived and practiced, won't apply to it.

Third, the towering figure in the psychology of cognitive development, as everybody knows, has been Jean Piaget. Piaget's own sense of what philosophy is belonged more to the Swiss and French culture in which he grew to maturity than to the dominant traditions in the English-speaking world. Philosophy on the continent has tended to be more pretentious and more systematic than it has in English-speaking countries. By contrast, the styles of analytic philosophy that have dominated the English-speaking world have been characteristically unpretentious. They have often included a remarkable playfuless and whimsy. (Lewis Carroll was, after all, a professional philosopher.) Such styles are much more closely akin to the kind of reflection young children are so readily capable of, and indeed, so very good at, than are the much more ambitious styles that Piaget took for a model. Not surprisingly, then, Piaget identified adolescence, his period of "formal operations," as the time when there would be sufficient intellectual stature and breadth of knowledge for philosophical thinking to emerge. Piaget himself showed almost no sensitivity toward or appreciation for or, I'm inclined to add, *patience with* the philosophical abilities of younger children, even though that ability sometimes shines through even his edited interrogatories sufficiently to warm the heart of an English-speaking philosopher. (See Chapter 4 of *Philosophy and the Young Child.*)

Is it important whether developmental psychology has anything much to say about the emergence in young children of the ability to engage in genuinely philosophical dialogue? In a way, I think, it is important, and in a way it isn't. Suppose it is not possible to arrive at a common understanding as to what maturity in philosophical thinking and discussion might consist in. Then perhaps this ability is not something developmental psychologists should be concerned with. Developmentalists have better things to think about, things that better suit the aims and strategies of their discipline.

But there is another side to this issue that must not be overlooked. Teachers and sophisticated parents look to developmental psychology for an expert's view of what their children are like, indeed, of what their children *should be* like. If there is no place in the developmentalist's story for the ability to enter into philosophical dialogue—perhaps because that ability doesn't lend itself to the developmentalist's research strategy—then many teachers and sophisticated parents will not think to engage their children in open philosophical discussion. Then neither the adults nor the children will have any acquaintance with that wonderfully strange mode of inquiry in which grown-ups cannot control the outcome or rely on the advantage of age and experience to maintain their position. And neither children nor adults will be able to enjoy the special thrill that comes when insight bursts unexpectedly on shared puzzlement and miraculously clears it away.

Epilogue

I ATTENDED A CONCERT given by St. Mary's Music School in the Queen's Hall, Edinburgh, in June 1983 to mark the end of the school year. Neil and David-Paul came over to sit with me.

Neil said he had just been reading the stories we had written together, a clean copy of which had been distributed to the children the week before. "They're good," he said and added, with a conspiratorial grin, "I'm just up to the bit about the dog piddling on the carpet."

"I remember you liked that part in class," I said.

After we sat down, I leaned over to David-Paul and said, "I keep thinking of things I would like to talk to you guys about."

"For instance?"

"Well," I said, looking at my program and thinking about the music we were soon to hear, "we could have a story in which somebody says that a certain bit of music is sad, and then someone else says that music can't be sad, it's *people* who are sad. Then maybe Freddie, after thinking about the matter for a while, suggests that sad music is music that is written by people when they are sad. Then maybe Alice hears this idea and says it can't be right. She takes, say, 'Frere Jacques,' and sings it in a fast and bouncy way." I sang it in a fast and bouncy style to illustrate. "Now Alice points out that you can take the very same tune, slow it down, and put it in a minor key, like *this*." Again, I sang the illustration.

"That would be like a funeral march," said David-Paul.

"Exactly," I replied, thinking of how Mahler makes a funeral march out of "Frere Jacques" in one of his symphonies. "Now . . ."

"I *like* doing that," said David-Paul.

"Now you wouldn't have to be sad to do that," I rambled on, "you could do it as an exercise or a game or something fun . . ." Only then did it occur to me that David-Paul had already made my point for me. "As you just said now," I added, rather feebly, "when you said you *liked* doing that."

"So it couldn't be that sad music is music written by people who are sad," David-Paul agreed.

"Would that be a good thing to talk about—what it is for some music to be sad and other music to be happy?" I asked.

He nodded. "There are so many things we could talk about."

I couldn't think of a nonsentimental response to that, so I just said, "Yes," lamely. We turned our attention to the concert, about which there was nothing at all sad and which, as I soon came to appreciate, was a splendid finale to my association with St. Mary's Music School.